For Pet's Sake,

Do Something!

Book One:
How to Communicate with Your Pets
And Help Them Heal

Dr. Monica Diedrich

For Pet's Sake, Do Something!

How to Communicate with Your Pets And Help Them Heal

Book 1 of the Do Something! Series

© 2006 Dr. Monica Diedrich. All rights reserved

ISBN 978-0-9713812-7-8

Published by:

Two Paws Up Press
P.O. Box 6107
Anaheim, CA 92816-6107
Email: drmonica@petcommunicator.com
Website: http://www.petcommunicator.com

Printed in the United States of America

Table of Contents

Table of Contents (cont'd.)

Introduction

"Where can pet parents go to find a compilation of information that will help them support their pets' various physical, emotional and spiritual needs?"

A frequently asked question in my practice—Dr. Monica

There usually comes a time toward the end of our pets' lives when we need to let go and let nature take its course. But in the face of most of the distresses and health challenges our pets encounter in daily living, we don't need to stand by crying helplessly and feeling sad. We can—*Do Something!*

Yet, where can pet parents go to find a compilation of information, which will help them support their pets' various physical, emotional and spiritual needs?

As I finished writing my second book, *Pets Have Feelings Too!*, it was this very question that impelled me to begin yet another book—one that would be a "how to" guide for everyone who wants to do everything they can to help their pets, especially when their pets are in distress or experiencing health challenges of any kind.

It all began with my desire to respond to the question, asked by so many of my clients and students over the years, "How can *I* talk with my pets?" But there were so many other topics which sprang to mind as I continued to write that before I knew it, I had enough material for a series of three "how to" books:

- *How To Communicate With Your Pets and Help Them Heal;*
- *How To Heal Your Pets Using Nutrition, Herbs and Supplements;* and
- *How To Heal Your Pets Using Alternative Therapies*

This, the first book in the series, begins by teaching you how to communicate with your pets about everyday things, as well as their health challenges. But discovering what your pets want to tell you is only the beginning. Once you're truly aware of their needs, you must then *Do Something*! That "something" usually involves restoring balance and harmony in their lives. So, the second part of the first book shows you how to use spiritual and energetic healing methods as one way to bring about that balance and harmony. There are also a series of guided meditations to enable you to help your pet cope with a variety of life situations.

The second book of the series covers the importance of nutrition, herbs and supplements, plus foods to avoid, and recipes for pets with special needs. The third book presents practical healing modalities including homeopathy, flower essences, incense, essential oils, crystals, color, sound, massage, magnets, hydrotherapy, acupressure, acupuncture and chiropractic, plus some other helpful guidance.

As I was writing all three books, I knew many readers would wonder what qualifies me to teach people how to communicate with and heal their animals. What experiences and training did I have that prepared me not only to do this, but also to teach others to do the same? To answer this question, I'd like to share a few of the highlights of my life with you.

I've known that I can understand what animals are saying ever since I was eight years old. However, when I was young, other children used to call me weird or crazy, and that was very painful. I didn't want to be different, so I tried hard to push aside the images animals were sending me and make believe I wasn't receiving them. But by my late teens, I began to realize that what I was experiencing was a gift—one that was becoming virtually impossible to ignore. So I nurtured this gift, and soon I grew more confident about using my abilities.

I began communicating with many different species of pets and was delighted to be able to help them and their humans better understand each other. In time, I realized that I'd taken the first step on the path of what I considered to be my Life Assignment.

But I'd also been searching for answers to many spiritual questions for the better part of my life. The answers to those questions came one at a time over several years. I read a lot of books and attended many classes.

One of those classes, offered by a Vietnamese gentleman, Master Tam Nguyen, would change the direction of the rest of my life and teach me how to use my intuitive gift more fully. From him, I learned that healing is about restoring balance and harmony, that healing is available to everyone, and that we can bring about healing for ourselves and for others.

During the last week of Master Tam's class, he was able to help me experience the Life Force Energy that always surrounds every living being. This loving, healing Light and Energy surrounded me in a way I'd never felt it before. When the class exercise was over, I was crying. For the first time in my life, I'd been able to *feel* this energy. It came charged with such Love that I felt God had just embraced me.

Master Tam approached me after class and encouraged me to continue to learn to let this loving, healing Energy flow through me for the benefit of others. He also invited me to come to his Center. I think I went the first time because I was curious, but I kept going back because I was learning so much about helping others to heal, not only spiritually, but also physically. I was drawn to return again and again.

Observing many healing experiences filled me with the desire to further deepen my knowledge and understanding of metaphysics, and it was this study that would gently lead me along the path of unconditional love. And what better way to express unconditional Love for someone than by bringing balance and harmony into their lives through healing.

Through Master Tam's teachings, I'd already been introduced to the technique of Cosmic Healing, which helps every living being function, as it should in perfect harmony with the Universe.

Cosmic Healing doesn't use any physical modalities like touch or medicine. Instead, it's done spiritually, from the heart, and with love. This type of healing requires direct communion with the Source of All Life, God, Spirit, Life Force, Supreme Being, All That Is.

In the process of learning to tune in to this loving, healing Energy, the skeptic in me reacted by asking, "If healing energy always surrounds everyone all the time, why isn't everyone accessing it more often? And why do we see so much sickness around us? What, if anything, can we do to bring healing to others, or to help people find healing for themselves?"

With patience and further experience, I began to understand that often, people in need of healing haven't learned to ask for help, or they feel they don't deserve it. Most of them know they want to be healed but they don't ask to be healed. They may not even know how to ask. So what should we do to find effective healing?

First, we need to believe that healing is possible, that it does take place, and that we can heal ourselves. We also need to have confidence that the healing energy of The Universe can flow through us, or flow to us through others.

Above all, the person needing healing, and the person helping, must take time to be in communion, or attunement, with the one true Source of All Life.

Then we must stop looking at the problem itself and start focusing on our connectedness to, and our oneness with, the Source of our Being, the Source of our balance and harmony. When we once again fully remember our oneness with Spirit, we're then able to manifest abundant good health for ourselves and for others.

For a number of years, I helped many people heal, and I communicated with many pets about everyday things, but I'd never thought about combining my gift for healing with my gift for communicating with animals. It was one of my own precious Shih-Tzus who would show me the way.

Chop Chop was only two years old when, one day, he was lying beside me with his eyes fixed somewhere on the horizon. He was giving up, and death seemed to be looming not many hours away from him.

Unable to think clearly, all I could do was to keep him company, crying because there didn't seem to be anything else I could do to help him. Two different veterinarians had already closely examined him. Medications were no longer effective, and the prognosis was very bleak. I lay on blankets on the floor next to him to give him what comfort I could.

But as I reclined there beside him on the floor, feeling very sad and miserable, he sent me a telepathic message just as clear as day: "You call yourself a healer. You've helped a lot of people. *So Do Something!*" He now looked me straight in the eye as he prompted me to be an active participant, not just a sorrowful bystander.

What he said to me kept playing over and over again in my mind until I finally got it.

His plea was very simple, yet I hadn't thought to use spiritual healing for him, or for other animals for that matter. I'd only used it to help people. But that was about to change.

He responded, literally overnight, to the first healing treatment I gave him, and within a week of continued treatments, he was completely back to being his normal happy self. You can read the full account of his story in Chapter 1 of my first book, **What Your Animals Tell Me.**

Thanks to the lesson Chop Chop taught me, I knew, then, that it was time to combine my gift for healing spiritually with my gift for communicating with animals. There were many other intuitives available to help heal people, so from then on, I resolved to dedicate my life exclusively to helping only animals.

My work now includes not only private consultations for pets, but also presenting classes, workshops and lectures, as well as doing extensive research, and writing books to share with others all that I've learned about how we can make life better for our beloved pets.

During the early part of my experience with Chop Chop, I could only cry, feel sorry for myself and for him, and wait for the inevitable. I felt completely inadequate, totally devoid of ideas, and utterly helpless.

Later on, it occurred to me that many pet parents often feel just as I did whenever they're faced with their pets' illnesses. But you don't need to go through those same feelings because there are so many things you can do, either to help your pets heal, or at least go through the process of their illness or pain with less discomfort. To help you, I've described as many healing modalities as possible in the three books of this series, **For Pet's Sake, Do Something!**

If you're able to ease your pet's pain, or provide quality of life for another day, week, month or even longer by implementing any of the healing techniques described in these books, your time and money spent on them will have been well worth it.

My teacher and beloved animal friend, Chop Chop, taught me that I didn't have to be a bystander. Thanks to him, when I was on the verge of giving up, I discovered instead that I could *Do Something!*

I hope you'll *Do Something* too. Healing can be brought about in many ways, not only for your pets, but also for yourself. When you're able to be an active participant in your pet's care, or bring peace and comfort to your pet because you've been able to *Do Something*, your spirit will also be healed.

Dr. Monica Diedrich
Anaheim, California, USA
November 2006

Chapter 1

The Importance of Intuition
And the Art of Meditation

What You Need to Know First to Be Able
To Communicate Effectively with Your Pet

Most of you who've been waiting for this book about communicating with your pets and helping them to heal may be tempted to skip the first two chapters and dive immediately into those that describe how to communicate with your pets. PLEASE DON'T! Or, if you absolutely can't resist taking a peek ahead, please let it be only a quick peek, and then come right back to the beginning of the book.

If you're going to learn how to use the techniques in Chapters 3 and 4 effectively, then at the very least, you're going to need to know something about the concepts presented in this chapter first. And understanding the information in the next chapter "Beyond Empathy," may also be very helpful for you.

In a nutshell, the first four chapters have been created to give you a sequential learning experience, so reading them in order is highly recommended.

With that said, let's talk now about The Importance of Intuition first, and then about The Art of Meditation.

Intuition. We all have it, but we're not always aware of it. It's a special sense of *knowing*. It's an inner feeling. It tells us that possibly something may be wrong, or it may be very right. Sometimes it's a sense of: don't board that plane, skip that planned event, turn around and go a different way; or make that phone call, go to a specific place, or wait just a little while longer before making that final decision.

It may even be knowing that you said just the right words at the right time, or knowing exactly what another person is going to say, just before they say it. How about feeling that something is wrong with a family member who's very far away, and finding out later that you were right? Or knowing who's on the other end of the line even before you pick up the phone?

Some of us experience these incidents with frequency, while others only do so on occasion. The fact is, we're all capable of putting our intuition to good use, but first, we must learn to listen to that quiet inner voice frequently enough to be able to recognize it.

This little voice inside of you is gently requesting—or perhaps insistently demanding—your attention. It speaks to you when you're awake, giving you information, sometimes subtly, and other times very clearly.

If you learn to follow your intuition, you'll find many rewards, but if not, you'll miss many opportunities. That's when you'll often find yourself saying, *"I Just Knew It,"* and subsequently regretting actions not taken.

Staying focused on your intuitive knowing requires practice, because thoughts flow in and out of your consciousness freely and effortlessly. You're here one minute, and the next you're mentally making your grocery list, or reliving a past experience. The key is to regularly, and gently, train yourself to be *mindful*.

When your attention moves quickly and randomly from thought to thought, like ripples in the waters of a lake, it produces constant motion in your consciousness, and then the reflection of your spirit can't be clear. When your thoughts are still, like the waters of a peaceful lake, with an agreeable sheen, your inner senses become heightened, almost as if you're in another plane of experience.

It's then that you're in attunement with the Source of All Life, and it's then when you're able to communicate spiritually with either another person or an animal. In these moments, it becomes easy to experience *their* feelings.

But attention doesn't like to be contained for extended periods of time; so again, you must consistently train yourself to be *mindful*.

How do you do this? How are you supposed to calm the inner chatter of your mind so that you can focus on your intuitive knowings?

The answer is: **Meditation**. Meditation is the art of non-thinking. It's that moment in time when the chatter subsides and our attention can then be focused on someone outside of ourselves.

And why is meditation so important? Because meditation enables you to develop your intuition—your capacity to see, to sense, to receive and to understand information that otherwise you'd be unaware of.

Meditation doesn't have to be done for long hours, or done in a state of special reverence. If you wish, you *may* use the traditional Chinese method of sitting on the floor with your legs crossed, though this is not usually a comfortable position for most westerners. Instead, just sit in a chair or on a sofa. I don't recommend meditating while lying on your bed, however, because you may become *so* relaxed that you'll fall asleep instead. Neither should the chair or sofa be too cushy!

During your meditation period, you're training your mind to "just be." To be in the moment and not to think about the list of things to do later today, or the list of things you've forgotten. Just be in the moment. This is often difficult for a person to do when they've never tried it before, but with practice you'll find yourself quieting the inner chatter in just a matter of moments.

People who find it difficult to quiet their minds need to do certain things to help themselves reach a relaxed state.
- Select a quiet place and time of day
- Always turn off the phones, and choose a place to sit which is away from any distractions
- If it's helpful, put on a guided meditation tape, or *very soft* calming music in the background.

The goal here is to have your mind so relaxed that instead of producing thoughts of your own, you're able to receive thoughts from someone else. This takes a lot of practice.

You may want to ask your animals to be with you during this time, or you may find that on their own, they'll gravitate to your space, because you'll look so peaceful to them in your inner relaxed state.

Beginning your meditation

Sit either on the floor in the traditional Chinese position, or sit relaxed in a chair or on a sofa, with your feet and legs uncrossed, and your hands on top of your legs, palms up.

If you prefer, you may put one hand on top of the other, palms up, with the tips of your thumbs touching each other.

If you experience distractions, you might visualize yourself sitting in a peaceful forested area near a flowing brook. As leaves go floating by in the water, put each distracting thought on a leaf, so that it can float downstream, out of sight and out of mind.

Or, picture a beautiful lacquered box with many drawers. Each time you have a distracting thought—"I forgot to go to the cleaners today," "I have to remember to bake cookies for the school event tomorrow," "I still have that report to write for work," etc.—put that idea into one of the drawers. You'll be sure to remember these thoughts again whenever you need to, because they're now securely tucked away and will be waiting for you once you finish your meditation.

Sit there for ten or fifteen minutes, no more.

Steps during meditation

Start with a deep, slow, satisfying breath (with your mouth closed). Hold it for a short while and then release it slowly. . . slowly. . . slowly.

Remember to begin your breath deep within your abdomen by pushing the stomach muscles out. Your abdomen should move outwards, *but your shoulders should be still.*

Then release all the air, by gently blowing it out through your slightly opened mouth, all the while tightening the muscles in your stomach. As you release your breath, make sure you let go of all of the tensions of the day.

Continue breathing in (mouth closed) and out (mouth slightly open), remaining aware of your stomach muscles, and being sure that your shoulders are *not* moving as you inhale.

If you're able to count during your intake and releasing of breath, you may find it much easier to stay in the moment.

The ideal timing is to inhale to a count of four, hold for a count of sixteen, and then slowly release for a count of eight.

However, many people need to start with a shorter counting pattern until they've practiced for quite awhile.

(Just a short, technical thought: Eventually, you want to achieve the ratio of holding your breath four times as long as it took you to inhale, and you want to release your breath for a count that's half as long as you held it, whatever count you're finally able to use.)

The *primary* point here is to learn to concentrate on, and control, your breathing, so start with *whatever* count works best for you, regardless of what it may be.

It needs to be a count that you're comfortable enough with so that you'll *willingly* do it *regularly*, even if that means only a count of four, four and four in the beginning.

You'll increase your capacity naturally as you practice.

With your breathing pattern established, start by mentally releasing all of your tensions each time you exhales. You may even feel your shoulders dropping and becoming more relaxed as you do this.

Make a conscious effort to imagine your stress and everyday concerns disappearing.

Tell yourself that every muscle in your body is completely relaxed, that every bit of tension is leaving your body every time you exhale.

With every breath you inhale, imagine the wisdom and tranquility of the Universe, like a soft glowing, loving light, infusing your lungs first and then infusing every cell of your body.

Tell yourself that there's only peace, comfort, ease and relaxation within you.

When you're first learning to meditate, simply remain in this relaxed state for up to fifteen minutes, releasing all thoughts and inner chatter, until you're attuned to the Source of All Life, and just enjoying the quietness.

When you're able to be in the "now state" for even a minute or two, you have indeed accomplished your goal. That means you are *not* thinking! You are just *being*!

Ending your meditation

Most beginners will simply find that their meditation ends naturally at about fifteen minutes. However, if you're simply

5

practicing meditation, and you're not going to communicate with your pet at the moment, you may tend to become *very* deeply relaxed.

If this is the case, you can consciously end your meditation by using a count of one to five as follows:

1. Be aware of feeling very relaxed, but ready to return to normal activity
2. Feel your breathing become more noticeable
3. Breathe even more naturally
4. Feel your body beginning to move and stretch
5. Eyes wide open now, refreshed and fully aware

A closing thought

Once you've experienced how to achieve a state of peaceful relaxation, you'll then be ready to communicate spiritually with your pets if you wish to do so. Chapters 3 and 4 will provide detailed information about how to do just that.

You'll also find much more in depth information about meditation and intuition in the upcoming chapters about spiritual and energetic healing. And the section on Guided Meditations will provide you with supportive guidelines that you may want to use when communicating with your pets, especially about health concerns.

Chapter 2

Beyond Empathy

Empathetic . . . or . . . Empathic?

Before you try to communicate with your animals, it's not only important to understand the concepts of intuition and meditation, but it's equally important to comprehend the difference between being empathetic (em-pa-the-tic), and being empathic (em-path-ic).

Empathy is the ability to *know with your mind, or spirit,* what others are feeling physically, emotionally, intellectually or spiritually. Almost everyone is *empathetic* towards others frequently during their lifetime. These feelings come quite naturally to anyone who cares.

But to be *empathic* (not just empathetic), is to *actually experience temporarily* in your own body, the very same feelings that belong only to someone else at the moment.

As you're helping your pets to heal physically, emotionally and spiritually, all of you will no doubt be relating to your pets with empathy, over and over again. But some of you, who have the gift of being an empath, as I do, may even be able to actually *experience* what your pets are going through.

If you're just now realizing that you do have empathic ability, you may find the idea somewhat disconcerting. You may have been asking yourself questions like: Am I crazy? Where did *those* feelings come from? What am I supposed to do with them? Are they mine, or are they my pet's? How can I turn them off? And how do I turn them on when I need to?

In this chapter, I'll share some of my personal *empathic* experiences with you and try to answer all of those questions, plus a few others. You'll find that you're not crazy, and you're not even particularly unique in this respect, because there are many others who also have this very special gift. And you'll learn how to turn your empathic feelings on and off at the appropriate times so that you can use them for a higher purpose, yet not be overwhelmed by them.

My own empathic experiences

I was born a natural empath, but for a very long time, I didn't understand that this was a special kind of gift. There was no one I knew who understood my gift, or could explain it to me, so when I had my first empathic experience, it was quite startling.

Visiting with my favorite aunt was always a special joy for me. In my young eyes, she was the perfect mother and homemaker. She even knew how to be my friend. And when I went to visit her, I also had two cousins to play with, which for an only child was a very special treat.

I must have been around nine years old, and my cousins were barely seven and five. On this occasion, we were having fun playing in their cozy apartment in the metropolitan city of Buenos Aires, Argentina. My uncle was busy reviewing some papers in the living room, my aunt was sewing and watching TV in one of the bedrooms, and we children were playing in the other bedroom. The game was hide-and-seek, and it was my turn to go look for the girls.

I went to the second bedroom where my aunt was, and momentarily looked at the program on the black and white television. I asked her what she was watching, and without taking her eyes off the set, she answered that she was about to watch an eye cataract operation performed by a new kind of doctor. As soon as she finished saying that, I turned to look at the screen, and I saw that a knife was inserted underneath the eyelid of the patient. The camera came in for a real close up. All you could see was one closed eyelid and the outline of the knife underneath that eyelid.

The journalist was talking about how the patient was not sedated and, in fact, was sitting upright in a chair, while the "surgeon" was conducting this miraculous operation by barely touching the man's eye. All I could see was the outline of the knife, now moving from one side of the eye to the other in a fast motion. There was no blood or discharge of any kind, no complaints of pain, in fact nothing exceptional at all.

I was paralyzed for a second, and very confused by the strange and powerful feelings in my body. It seemed to me as if I was experiencing what the man having the surgery on TV was feeling, but I didn't know how to cope with those feelings. It wasn't painful. It was just strange, and for whatever reason, I understood clearly that the feeling was not coming from within me, but that it was his. I stood there for a couple of seconds and then, disturbed by my body's reaction, I turned to leave the room.

That's all I remember about the peculiar feeling in my body. The next thing I knew, I was on a bed, but I didn't know why. My aunt explained that I'd fainted and hit my head on the doorknob when I fell. My hand instinctively reached up to feel the large swollen bump on my forehead, and I tried to understand what had happened. Meanwhile, my aunt frantically searched for some salts or alcohol for me to smell so that she could get me up and about again.

I remember she asked me what had happened, as if I'd done it on purpose. When I told her how uncomfortable I felt watching the image on TV, she dismissed it by saying that I shouldn't watch those things because I was too sensitive. She later told my mother what had happened, and from then on, I was shielded from anything remotely painful or frightening, like blood, accidents or pain of any kind. I wasn't allowed to watch such things on TV, nor even see them in real life. In fact, I'd never been around the sick or dying, or even attended a funeral, until after I was married and my husband's grandmother passed on.

Consequently, I always thought I lacked the ability to handle painful situations. I used to pray that if anything happened to my children, my husband would be around to help, because I thought I'd be useless and unable to deal with the situation. Of course, as it turned out, he wasn't always able to be there.

Often when the boys were growing up and got hurt, there were many times when it was completely up to me to take care of them, bandage their cuts, soothe their pain, or take them to the hospital with split foreheads, chins, or broken arms. Every single time, although I felt ready to pass out myself, I somehow managed to rise to the occasion.

It never occurred to me until much later in life that what I was feeling in all of these experiences was a special form of empathy. *Their* pain had become my pain, but I hadn't realized that yet. Eventually, I simply became used to temporarily experiencing those feelings within my own body, whether they were emotional or physical.

But, over time, I discovered that I was experiencing these feelings *because* of my empathic gift, so I then began to learn how I could more comfortably live with this special gift, and how to use it more effectively.

My natural abilities as an empath had given me so much discomfort, especially when I was young, that I usually preferred to stay away from pain so that I wouldn't have to go through the experience of it. Yet, all I needed to do was to learn how to manage it by turning the "switch" on and off.

And how could I do that? I finally discovered that the best way for me to handle the intense feelings of others was to practice detachment. For me, detachment meant that I had to do one of two things whenever my physical boundaries were compromised by being too close to someone who was experiencing pain, emotionally or physically.

The most obvious thing to do was to leave their company, but sometimes that wasn't possible. My other option was to learn to detach myself from *their* feelings by understanding that they were *their* feelings, and not mine. Through trial and error, over a period of many years, I became reasonably proficient in the art of detachment. Unfortunately, in certain circumstances, I still occasionally struggled to regain my own feelings of well-being. This was true when I used to work with people, and it was also true when I began to work exclusively with animals.

By the time I devoted myself to giving animals a voice, I was already a fairly skilled empath, but when I found myself helping at a chiropractic clinic for pets, my work with animals, and my empathic gift, both took quite a unique turn.

It was the prompting of my chiropractor colleague which showed me how I could fine tune my empathic abilities even further, and working together with her provided an incredible number of opportunities to regularly practice the art of detachment.

When she treated animals, the chiropractor needed to find out exactly where their pain was located and how a specific bone or nerve was affecting different parts of their bodies. Since animals can't speak, she relied on me to give her the answers. Her questions to the animals were very specific. Where does it hurt? Does the pain feel different now when I touch you here? How is your neck feeling? How does your stomach feel? Are you able you relieve yourself? Does it hurt when you urinate? Can you feel your tail? Does the pain travel, or does it stay in one place? Can you feel you legs, your feet, your toes?

When she first started asking these questions, I almost laughed out loud. "You want me to ask them *that*?" I said.

"Yes," she'd reply, in her matter-of-fact tone. "Ask them! They should be able to tell you." Since I had nothing to lose, I did ask. And guess what! They *knew*, and they *could* tell me. I'd *feel* their answers delivered immediately into my own body. I'd allow my body to feel and to linger in the pain long enough so that I could explain, in detail, where it was located and how it felt. Sometimes it was a pain that was concentrated in one area, and sometimes it was pain that could be felt all over the body. Other times, the animals would tell me that a medicine made them feel nauseated or didn't agree with their systems in general. I even felt the emptiness of miscarriage, as in the case of Sophie, the goat, whose story appeared in my second book, *Pets Have Feelings, Too*!

Soon my chiropractor associate and I had a routine. She'd ask me questions while she worked on the animal. I'd have my eyes closed and concentrate on the locations and the feelings, and I'd explain, to the best of my ability, what I felt and where I was feeling it. She'd then proceed to adjust the animal. If I felt a release of pain right away, my eyes would open and I'd be feeling good again. Other times, no matter how much she tried, the pain would persist.

This empathic process was fascinating, but the most important thing I was learning, whenever I was using it, was to detach as soon as my eyes would open. I'd no longer feel the pain and, because I *had* detached, I was able to move to the next room and do it all over again with the next patient.

Sometimes, though, it got to be too much, even for me. I remember that, after one intense morning at the clinic, my associate and I decided to go out to lunch to relax a bit. In the middle of our lunch hour, we received a call from the animal hospital requesting our help. When we arrived, the animal (a dog) was already lightly sedated and waiting for the able hands of the chiropractor to make an adjustment. The dog had injured her back while playing.

The chiropractor asked me to describe the pain or discomfort and I immediately became aware of feeling excruciating pain. I also felt overcome with nausea. I answered as many questions as I could, but made a hasty exit as soon as I was able, fearing that otherwise my lunch would make an unwanted appearance.

As soon as I walked out of the building, I felt fine again. It took me a few more moments, though, to realize that *I* wasn't the one who had been feeling nauseated. Instead, what I was empathically feeling was the nausea that the dog was experiencing from the numbing sedative she'd been given. I'd now detached from that feeling by going outside, and the dog would be fine again when the sedative wore off. But most importantly, I clearly realized once again that, even though the feelings were intense, they were those of the animal, and not mine.

Medical intuitive or medical empath?

These two terms are sometimes used interchangeably, though just as there's a difference between being empathetic (able to understand in mind or spirit what someone else is feeling) and being empathic (actually experiencing in one's own body what someone else is feeling), there's also a difference between being a medical intuitive and being a medical empath.

In her book, *Empowered by Empathy*, Rose Rosetree distinguishes between the two in simple terms. "A Medical Intuitive," she says, "is a Psychic who specializes in receiving health-related information. With an objective understanding, they read the client's problems. Energetically, they stay within their own personal boundaries. A Medical Empath energetically merges into their clients. They too impart diagnostic information, but their means of gaining knowledge is more personal."

While I'm an empath, the point I want to make is, that no matter what "label" you use to define my work, I know what the animals are feeling and I'm able to describe those feelings because I can experience them happening in my own body.

If you want to learn more about whether or not you may be an empath, I highly recommend you read Rose's book. She teaches everything you ever wanted to know about being an empath. It's a fascinating, hands-on explanation of how to differentiate between who you are and what your unique gifts are.

As I see it, in the not too distant future, empaths will work hand-in-hand with veterinarians. We'll be able to assist them by providing information they wouldn't otherwise be aware of. This, in turn, will enable them to more effectively help many animals, especially those who have conditions that are particularly difficult to diagnose.

But for now, with very few exceptions, animal communicators are relegated to work outside the veterinary community because many in the traditional medical field tend to view this, and any other alternative modality of healing, as unscientific, inefficient, and ineffective.

Yet, we need to incorporate all of our senses whenever we're dealing with a medical issue. Empathy can make us feel connected with another being at a certain level of understanding, but empathic feelings, because they're experienced at an entirely different level, can play an essential role when it comes to helping veterinarians arrive at a medical diagnosis.

Almost all medical professionals, and even skeptics, have hunches that they follow up on without questioning where they came from. And often they've discovered that the only way they were able to solve the problem was by following those intuitions. As more and more veterinarians realize how intuitive feelings can help them be more effective caregivers, I'm certain that empaths and veterinarians will begin to work much more closely together.

The empathic gift—turning it on, turning it off, and letting go

You, too, may already know that you have an empathic gift. Or maybe, by reading this book, you're just discovering, for the first time, what it is that you've been experiencing for so long. Or, maybe you've never even thought you were empathic, but now you'd like to find out if possibly you, too, can develop that ability. At whatever stage you find yourself, I want to help you understand how to manage this gift effectively.

It can be very difficult when you have strange feelings and you don't understand where they're coming from, or how to put them into words. Moreover, you don't even know who to talk to because you feel so *different*. Please take heart and know that there is nothing wrong with you.

After reading about my experiences, you now know that if you're actually able to *experience* the feelings of someone else, those feelings belong to *them*. They're *not* yours. You're just experiencing them temporarily. This wonderful ability to *feel* can be used to help others, but it's essential that you also learn to detach yourself from those feelings when they've served their purpose.

Before I learned to detach from them, my empathic feelings could actually be quite frightening. As a child and a young adult, finding myself engulfed by someone else's pain or emotions made me feel out of control. Having those empathic feelings "on" all the time is what's frightening, so you need to know how to "turn the switch on" when you want to do so, and, just as important, you must know how to "turn it off."

First, let's talk about switching it ON

Let's say that a friend approaches you with a sick animal and asks you to see if you're able to "receive any information." This is one way to describe what you might to do:

1. Sit down next to the animal and wait until he or she quiets down.

2. Do a brief meditation using some deep breathing techniques.

3. Your mind needs to be free from worries, like a blank slate, and your body must be relaxed and free from all tension.

4. Make sure you can identify any physical discomfort of your own because you don't want to associate your pain with the animal's pain or discomfort. If you do have some discomfort of your own, make a mental inventory first. Know what pain or discomfort is yours *before* you energetically move into the animal's body.

5. You may touch the animal, if you wish, by placing a single hand on top of his or her back, below the shoulder blades, right above the stomach area. This is the seat of the solar plexus and emotional aura on animals. (Note that I said place your hand *on top* of the back, and not underneath on the stomach. The corresponding chakra or energy center, which for humans is located on the abdomen near the stomach, is located on top of the body for animals, about halfway between the neck and the hips. This is depicted in a diagram in the chapter about Chakras.)

6. As you listen, you'll gradually start receiving important information from the pet in your own body.

7. Take an inventory of the pet's body by observing your own body. Start at the top of the pet's head and work slowly downwards. You can observe the external body first, and then check the internal organs. (There's a detailed description that explains how to take a physical inventory of a pet in Chapter 4.)

8. You can say out loud what your feelings are if someone else is there to record them for you or if you're using a tape recorder, or you can keep a written journal as you go.

9. When you're finished, take a deep breath, say thank you, and release the pain and discomfort your body feels. This is a *very* important step because you must cleanse your body of the animal's pain and feelings that you were temporarily experiencing. You can use any method that works for you. You might want to try

imagining a very efficient vacuum that's turned on and working on top of your head. It's a very special type of vacuum because it not only sucks out, and *totally* removes, all feelings of disease or pain, but it then converts that negative energy back into the energy of love.

10. Open your eyes. Feel refreshed, and glowing with the healing energies of the Universe.

Next, we need to look at how to switch the feelings OFF

If, in the beginning, you find it difficult to simply disconnect, you can try several other techniques:

1. Change environments. If you're inside your home, go to your favorite room and contemplate how good it feels to be there. Or, go outside and take a walk enjoying the flowers, or your surroundings. It's particularly helpful to observe the peacefulness and beauty of nature. Or, go to your car and listen to your favorite music station, talk show or CD. You can either simply sit in the car, or go for a drive.

2. If these quick "fixes" aren't working, go elsewhere. Go shopping. This, of course, is my favorite one! Not necessarily because I like to shop so much, but because for me, shopping is a wonderful release for my mind. When I'm enjoying the things I'm seeing, searching for just the right item, or looking for the perfect gift for someone, I'm able to disconnect from all bothersome thoughts, and let my mind fully relax.

3. Do a relaxing meditation with any self-help audiotape or CD. Take a bath. Light some candles.

You can try these and many other things and you'll eventually find what works best for you. The main theme here is to detach from what you've been feeling, and reconnect with yourself for a short while. You've "worked" for someone else and it's now time to "work" for you. Now, so to speak, "It's all about *me*." My husband laughs when I'm in this phase of my work but, because he's experienced it for so many years, he understands my need. He's even teased me by buying me the Toby Keith CD entitled "I Wanna Talk About Me."

Keep in mind however, that as with most things, if you're an empath, there are no absolutes. Sometimes you'll *unintentionally* feel another's pain or emotions. If someone very sick or distressed gets too close to your aura, you may pick up the vibration right away and your internal alarm will go off. This is your personal warning system, like an alarm going off when someone gets too close to your car. Stop and listen. Understand that it's not *your* feelings that you're experiencing in your body. It's the feelings of the other person (or animal) who's with you.

To see if what you're feeling agrees with what they're experiencing, tell the person what you're feeling. Then ask how they feel and have them share information about themselves with you. Inquire if they've gone to see a doctor, or if they're taking any medicine. Understand how your body is identifying the specific pain. Is it an emotional hurt, a physical pain or a disease? You need to observe how your body reacts and how it feels, so that you can relate to another's pain, learn from it, and hopefully be able to help them.

Then you must let it go

If the pain is coming from an animal, and you're concerned about his or her health, trust your judgment. Don't hesitate. See to it that the pet receives veterinary attention right away. If it's your pet, explain to your vet what it is that you feel. If it's someone else's pet, give them a clear explanation that they can share with their veterinarian. Don't worry about the vet's reaction. That's not important compared with the health of a pet.

Sometimes an animal will send you a spontaneous message, even when you haven't been asked to communicate with him or her. In this case, make sure you immediately let their human know what it is that the pet is telling you. It might be the only chance the animal has to be helped. You must do what you can, and *then let it go*.

Do **not**, I repeat, do **not** take it home with you. Do **not** let it bother you. Know that you did the right thing. It was *your* role to make someone else *aware* of the feelings you were getting. That's all. *Your responsibility* is to tell someone what you feel, and *then let it go.*

Once again, it's very important when you receive these feelings that you do *act* on them. Do whatever you feel is best at that moment. Do something, whether or not it seems significant, rather than doing nothing. Don't wait until later to voice those feelings. Then it may be too late.

If you have a gift for helping others, voicing those feelings is an expression of that gift. You were chosen for this purpose. "Chosen by whom?" you may ask. By your Higher Self, God, Spirit, The Divine, All That Is. But you need to understand that this is not something that was imposed on you. You were not a bystander in this choice. You agreed, at a spiritual level, to accept this gift. Now that you understand this, you can go forward in peace and love.

One of my very empathetic clients told me that she couldn't do what I do because she'd be crying all the time from "listening" to everyone's problems. She asked me once how I could possibly walk around a park or an animal shelter.

When I talked with her about the importance of detachment, she knew exactly what I was describing. She said that she'd also worked on detachment during a particularly trying time in her life, using some very helpful mental imagery. She'd imagine that all the pain and anger that belonged to another person would become a very heavy stone that she no longer chose to carry. She imagined herself taking this stone and throwing it down as she continued to walk away, without looking back, knowing that the burden was removed from her. Try this. It might just work for you.

Spiritual protection

One other point that many of my students ask about is how to protect themselves.

I'm not the best person to respond to this question because I don't feel there's anything I need to protect myself from. There's no way of contracting the disease from my animal clients just by feeling what they feel. There are no psychically contagious diseases that I need to be concerned about. But that's just me. I know they can't affect me, and therefore I don't need to be protected from them.

However, there are several things you can do if this is a concern for you:

1. Spend time in prayer, knowing that the love of God/Goddess/All that Is, is your protection and your shield.

2. In your meditation, invoke the help of the angels. They've been given to us to help protect us. Be specific in your request. Ask for protection, and also for help in receiving accurate information. *Always ask that everything be for the highest good of all.*

3. At the beginning of your prayer or meditation before a session, surround yourself with healing light before you start feeling the animal's pain or distress. Allow a shimmering white light to enter the top of your head and bathe your body from head to toe.

4. Burn sage or other incense in the area where you work with a client.

5. Burn candles of different colors representing different intentions. Like our chakras, the colors of candles are associated with different intentions; for instance, pure white represents healing and protection.

Except for prayer, none of the above actions has any power in or of itself, but each one can serve as a reminder to help you remain centered, so that you can focus on being of help to others.

You're not alone

Above all, what I want you to understand is that you're not alone in feeling the way you feel, and in your ability to "receive" information from either your pets or from animals in general (or maybe even from people).

When I was young, I thought I might be crazy. My cousins told me so. They said I was weird, just because I was different. Whoever heard of little girls talking with pets? Indeed, in this respect, I felt out of step with the rest of the world.

For years I didn't say anything to anybody because I thought I was so different and because nobody seemed to understand. I didn't know who to talk to. Grownups couldn't hear the animals speaking. They couldn't feel their pain. I could, but why did it happen only to me? *Was* I going crazy? I thought so for the longest time. Now, of course, I know that this is my gift.

Since a gift is always for giving, using mine became my Life Assignment. I wanted to share my special gift by helping animals communicate with their humans. I also discovered that I could share my gift with others through writing books.

I've received a lot of letters from people, both younger and older, especially after the release of my first book, **What Your Animals Tell Me.** They were people who were confused about their empathic skills and what to do with them. And they were often people who, for the very first time, discovered that there was actually someone out there who could understand them.

The first letter I'd like to share with you came from a fifteen-year-old girl. She'd received only a fifteen-minute consultation about one of her pets, with no time to talk about anything else. Her name has been omitted for privacy purposes, but here's the touching letter she wrote after we met:

Dr. Monica,

Hi, I met you at Whole Foods Market during a puppy fair and you saw me and my Jack Russell terrier. I also have three cats, two birds and two rabbits.

I wanted to tell you that when I was little, about age seven, I went to my Grandmother's friend's farm. She had horses, chickens, donkeys, sheep, barn cats, and four Huskies. She also babysat up to fifteen different dogs at times.

I'd go for one week every summer, and I'd be lying down in the field with this pack of dogs. I'd lie down on my favorite dog's huge belly and talk to her. Then one day I was thinking of what toy was her favorite toy, and suddenly the image of a chew toy popped into my head, so I went to retrieve it for her.

The next summer I returned. I sat with one of the dogs and was thinking that her leg must hurt because earlier she'd been limping. All of a sudden a huge pain went down my leg to my ankle, and a picture of her falling off the roof of the cabin that she loved to climb on came into my head. I instantly started crying and my Grandmother's friend, Diana, came to see what was wrong.

After a few minutes the pain faded away and I stopped crying. I told Diana what had just happened -- that I was wondering if the dog's leg was OK and that the dog had showed me her pain. Diana scolded me, and I was punished by having to clean the horse's pen for one week, and for a nine year old that was a huge punishment.

After that, I'd promised her that I wouldn't do it again, but I've done it twice in the last six years. I don't know how to control it. I want to be just like you, being able to use this gift, but I don't know how to summon it, because usually, without trying, it happens. I just read your book and it's wonderful and so enlightening to me. I've been trying the methods that you said to use. Please help. Thank you so much and I apologize for such a long letter.

Poor girl! She had no one to ask until now. All children need to be allowed to have the opportunity to express special feelings, and still feel accepted, even if we don't understand those feelings ourselves. *We also need to understand that, just because we can't do something unusual, it doesn't mean others can't do it.* How shortsighted and small-minded we've become! *Just because one person doesn't fit into the box of someone else's perception, it doesn't make that person wrong.*

Well, perhaps this poor girl had difficulties because of her youth, and the fact that the grownups in her life wouldn't listen to her. You might think it would be easier if you were older, right? Not so, as this second letter shows!

Dr. Monica,

I'm a 36-year-old woman and I have strange and disturbing things to tell you. I'll try to sum it up as fast as I can. I've loved animals all of my life. I currently have two dogs, a turtle, hermit crabs, fish, a guinea pig and a horse. I'm also going to college to earn a B.S. in Wildlife Biology so that I can work to rehabilitate injured wildlife and conserve their natural habitat.

But lately, probably the past two years, I've noticed that I feel so overwhelmed by strong feelings of sadness, or even pain, when I see any animal who is sad, depressed, neglected or dying. I mean it goes beyond sympathy and even beyond empathy. Sometimes I feel physically ill and sometimes I can't shake the feeling no matter what. Like just now, on my way home from work, I saw the car in front of me hit a raccoon and I felt so unbelievably terrible. I wanted to do something about it but I knew I couldn't. Now, two hours later, the feeling is still stuck with me.

Sometimes these feelings affect my daily routine or bother me at work. It's starting to drive me crazy because I wonder if I'm nuts. Sometimes I just want to cry. I might just be a neurotic weirdo. What do you think? I couldn't even kill mice when they were in my house. I'd trap them on glue traps, then set them free in the woods. What can I do about this? Is it my job in this lifetime to carry this burden? I want to use my love and empathy for animals to help them when they need it, but sometimes it seems to be too much for me. Sometimes I feel depressed for them. Please help me if you can. Tell me what you think I should do. I would really appreciate it if you could find the time to answer my questions. I don't know who else to ask. Thank you.

My answer went something like this:

Dear J:

I'm so happy you found me and decided to ask me your questions. I wish more people had a way to do so. When you have these experiences, it's sometimes difficult to put your questions into words. But once you're able to ask someone else who's had similar experiences, and who's willing to listen and help, then all of your misconceptions should vanish.

I'm here to tell you that you aren't sick or weird. You may not even be unique in what you're experiencing, but you do have a GIFT that not many people acquire in a lifetime of trying. Your gift has a name. You're an empath. I should know, since I also have that gift.

This ability connects you to another being, whether human or animal, at a deeper level than just using your mind to decide if something is painful or would make you feel sad. You actually feel *it in your own body; your senses become more aware of what you "feel" emotionally—be it sadness, pain, distress or fear. It's normal for an empath to feel exactly what the other being feels.*

In my case, for instance, I'd bend over in pain, or start to cry for no reason at all when I was around an animal in pain. It took me a long time (without anyone's help, mind you) to realize what was happening to me. But after awhile, I could actually observe each feeling, one at a time, and be able to help the animal.

I think one of the first things you need to work on is remembering that it's not you who is sick or sad or in fear. You're simply mirroring an emotion or other feeling that's being transmitted to you by another being in distress.

Your job is to try to help animals by using the information they're providing. You do the very best you can, then you must RELEASE IT. Just as doctors who see patient after patient in pain cannot take the burden home with them, so you should NOT take the burden home with you.

Do you understand how important this last sentence is? If you cannot do that, YOU WON'T BE ABLE TO HELP THE ANIMALS. But you're serious about your desire to help, so consider your empathic gift something to be used regularly in your LIFE'S WORK. It is a gift, but it's also a bit of a burden that we must joyfully carry with us as we go through life being of service to others (the animals) who don't speak our language.

Please keep in touch,

Dr. Monica

From this client's letter, it's easy to see how distressed she was by her unexplained ability to feel the pain of animals. But it's important to note that her distress came from being confused about why and how this happens. She needed to understand the role of an empath. I'm sure that once she had an understanding of how she could use her abilities to help the animals she wanted to protect, her fear was replaced by confidence in knowing that she's fulfilling her Life Assignment. There can be no greater satisfaction than that—I should know!

A closing thought

Now that you have an understanding of intuition and meditation, as well as knowing the difference between what it means to be empathic and empathetic, you're ready to learn, in the next two chapters, about how to communicate with your pets.

Chapter 3

Communicating With Your Pets About Everyday Things

The two questions almost all of my students and clients ask are: "How can I communicate with my own pets?" and "If I want to learn to communicate with animals, where do I begin?"

First, you need to understand the concepts of intuition, meditation and empathic experiences that were introduced in Chapters 1 and 2. Those first two chapters provide you with the foundation you need to effectively use the information you're now going to read about in Chapters 3 and 4.

So where *do* you begin?

The role of intuition

You must first recognize what an important role your intuition plays in talking with animals.

You also need to understand that the information you're going to receive in this new way of communicating will come to you not only from *seeing* intuitively, but also from *hearing and sensing* intuitively as well.

You must trust your intuition, and know that your Higher Self is in charge. It works only for your highest good, and also guides you to bring about the highest good for others.

And always, always remember that the answers to any of your questions are in your *first* thought, your *first* feeling, your *first* intuitive knowing.

Practical thoughts about talking with your pet

One essential thing to remember is that you have to *remove yourself and your own preferences from the picture.* What *you* feel about life in general makes no difference here. *Your* preferences for food, shelter, relationships, colors, sights, sounds, music, etc., must not be allowed to influence the information you receive.

Be absolutely honest with yourself about what you're seeing, hearing, feeling or sensing. Our animals are the most honest creatures in the world. They do not lie, so don't try to change anything they convey to you into something **you** think they should be saying.

Another important point is to *treat your animals with respect* when you're communicating with them. Ask them, don't just tell them. Express your questions or comments by giving your pets a reason why they should do something.

For example, if they need to lose weight, don't just say, "As of tomorrow, you're going on a diet." Tell them, instead, that you're going to be changing the way they eat so that, by losing some extra weight, they'll be able to walk or run more easily, or that it will be better for their heart and general health, or that losing weight may help them live longer. They may be more accepting of your ideas if you explain why something will be better for them, or why it's important to you.

You're going to need to be able to record the pictures and feelings you receive, so have paper and pen or a tape recorder handy before you begin your meditation.

Whenever a client is present with his or her pet, I simply describe my feelings to that person right at the moment. But when I'm working alone, I always write down the information I'm receiving so that I'll remember everything when the time comes to talk with the client. If you're working alone, you can either write your feelings and perceptions in a journal or speak them into a tape recorder, whatever works best for you.

However, if you don't take the time to write down, or record out loud, what you experienced, you won't be able to remember every single detail. And the answers lie in the details.

Your pet may be in the same room with you when you talk, but it isn't essential. You're going to be having a spiritual, heart to heart communication, not a body to body communication. For that reason, you can talk to your pet when you're traveling, when he or she is staying at the vets, or when your pet's outdoors and you're inside.

Some people are very visual and able to receive a "film clip" during the time they're communicating with their pets. Be aware of the information contained in any pictures you see, but don't necessarily expect to hear a sound track with it. Sometimes you will, and sometimes you won't.

You're not supposed to anticipate what the next answer will be like, or how it will come to you. However, when you're receiving information, and it's flowing quickly, you might almost be expecting one thing to come next, but discover that you get something entirely different. Be receptive to *everything*—colors, lights, sounds, smells, or simply an inexplicable knowing—because all of your senses are receiving at this moment.

Sometimes you might even notice a slight discomfort in your own body if your pet tries to tell you she's not feeling very well at the moment. Or you might see, hear or feel something that makes you cry or laugh! You might even hear a voice, or a whole sentence in a "voice" you don't recognize. And by the way, I don't want you to think you're crazy if you do!

Some of my pet clients not only send me their spiritual "voice," but with it I often get a special glimpse of their personalities. For instance, I remember a Boxer talking with a "Goofy" voice using the same pauses and expressions. An elderly Maltese sounded to me as if she were talking in an old woman's raspy voice (like someone who'd had too much to drink, and a smoke or two just before our talk). A beautiful young poodle sounded just like a southern young lady, including the southern accent and drawl, and a little Chihuahua talked with a lisp!

As you're doing your work with a pet, there'll no doubt be several things like this that will make you smile, along with those things that bring feelings of discomfort.

When you first start talking with your pet, the pictures the two of you send back and forth will usually have something to do with what your pet wants to tell you, or what you want to tell your pet, about everyday things. Later on, you may also want to communicate with your pet about the state of his or her health, which we'll talk about in Chapter 4.

The role of meditation

Before you invite your pet to engage in a conversation with you, the first thing you need to do is to quiet your own internal chatter, as you learned to do in Chapter 1, "*The Importance of Intuition and The Art of Meditation.*"

Set aside all the worries of the day, the shopping list, the errands to run, and the plans for dinner or entertainment. Focus on your animal using your whole mind, body and spirit.

When you're ready, close your eyes. Then begin by gently breathing and meditating until your mind is clear. Feel the love you have in your heart for your pet.

Having a conversation

Next, in your meditative state, with your eyes still closed, ask your pet to come close to you in your mind's eye. As she's approaching you, notice how well you're able to see the color and texture of her fur. Observe the expression in her eyes. Are her ears up or down, and do they move when she walks? Is her tail wagging, happy to see you, or is her tummy almost dragging on the floor? When she's approaching you, is she calm, excited, sad, agitated, moving slowly or quickly? Make sure to see every detail. Remember, your eyes are closed and you're seeing this picture in your mind and heart.

Once your pet is close to you in your mind's eye, picture how she sits in front of you as you touch her. Feel the fur in your hands as you mentally move your hand over her body. Is it silky? Does it give you comfort? Do you feel the love in her eyes? Do you feel your love flowing out to your pet? Make a bridge of light from your heart to your pet's heart. Send her your love by picturing a ray of golden light flowing from your heart to hers.

Now that you have her attention spiritually, you first want to receive any information your pet wants to share with you. This is the time for you to *listen* to what she says.

If you don't sense something right away, remain very relaxed, with your eyes closed, letting your mind be free of any thoughts.

Ask her if there's anything she'd like to tell you before you start asking her any questions. Listen attentively, and become aware of anything you see, hear, smell, sense or feel. If you receive something, talk with your pet about it.

After you feel she's finished telling you what was on her mind, then tell your pet that you'd like to ask her some questions. We'll discuss some specific topics you may want to inquire about in just a few moments.

But, first, how are you going to receive answers to your questions?

Let's revisit the topic of your intuition -- the soft voice you hear from deep inside. As soon as you've put your full attention on your pet, you must be ready to start receiving information intuitively.

Don't let your reason get the upper hand, which is what we often tend to do. If reason does get the upper hand, then thinking logically or rationally can silence what would otherwise come to you intuitively. Your inner voice is trying to tell you something. *Do not* discard this privileged information, and definitely *do not* underestimate its value. It will be your guide to right action. Trust your intuition.

Being open to receive information by meditating daily is the way to get started, but *you must also be coming from a sense of Love deep within your heart* or the information you receive may not be clear and accurate.

It's also essential that you learn to *detach from any input, other than what you are "reading" or sensing.* This means that you must not mentally judge the information coming from your inner voice, nor emotionally react to it. Just stay connected to your heart to know if what you're sensing is true.

When you're communicating with your pets, it may help to visualize the exchange of pictures as a moving stream that flows from your heart center to theirs. Notice how much love you feel and how clear the feelings become. Receive them, acknowledge them, and reciprocate them.

These messages, and their method of delivery, will come in an individual way. It will be unique to you. Some people see images, some hear words, others just sense things. Accept your way as the perfect one for you.

But *how*, exactly, do I ask my pet a question and HOW do I tell her about something important I want her to know, or do?

This is one of the most common questions I'm asked. I do it so automatically that I don't even think about the details any more. However, because so many people have requested very specific guidance, I'll provide several scenarios to help you get started.

Let's begin with simple things.

Let's say I want to ask my pet which food she prefers . . .

In your mind's eye, during the meditation time, visualize the bowl the animal usually eats from. Make the image distinct and precise. Picture the exact size and shape of the bowl in its regular location. See the bowl empty. Keep that image clear in your mind and wait. Usually the response will be immediate. You may now see the bowl with a certain kind of food in it, or you might smell it, taste it, or hear a word describing it. The answer may come to you so fast that you barely have time to grasp it, and then the whole picture's gone. If you're not certain about what you saw, ask your pet to show it to you again.

Or, try a different approach. This time "become" your pet for a moment. Almost as if you're putting on a suit, make yourself as big or as small as your animal, and look at the empty bowl through her eyes. Can you see a color, a shape, a quantity? Can you smell it? What is it? Ask her: Are you hungry? What food makes your mouth water in anticipation? Are you getting enough or too much to eat? Do you need more food, or do you just want more food because you like it so much?

If the image doesn't make sense right away, don't dismiss it. It might be that your pet needs to tell you that she's missing something in her diet, as she may do by showing you a picture where she's eating grass or licking a stone.

The above exercise is basically the same when you need to ask any question regarding a pet's favorite activities, toys, pastimes, sleep accommodations or friends.

Let's try something else now.

How do I get my pet to do something specific that I want him or her to do?

Whenever you're communicating with a pet, *always use positive statements.* Most people start their requests by saying something to their pet like, "I don't want you to do . . ." or, "I want you to stop doing . . .."

Animals do not clearly understand negative statements. Humans rely on words to communicate ideas, and we can use either positive or negative words. But animals do not comprehend negatives in the same way. When you say, "No!" in a loud voice, they may know you're angry and they may become fearful, and may even stop doing what you don't want them to do, but *they're reacting to your tone of voice, not to the words you're saying.* This is why, when you're trying to communicate with an animal, you must keep it in very simple terms, and what's even more important, *you must present every request as a positive statement.* Tell your pet what you *want* him to do, not what you don't want him to do.

For example:

- *Don't get on the couch,* should be: I like it when you lie on your blanket on the floor beside the sofa.
- *Don't claw the couch,* should be: You have your very own scratching post. That's the only place you should sharpen your nails.
- *Don't bite,* should be: Keep your mouth closed. Your teeth are sharp and they give us pain.
- *Don't pee or poop on the carpet,* should be: (Cats) Only use your litter box to do your business. I'll clean it for you every day. (Dogs) Only go pee and poop outdoors where there's grass or dirt (or cement, if that's all there is).
- *Don't jump,* should be: Keep your feet on the floor when you come to greet me. I'll show you how happy I am when you do that.

- *Don't chew my belongings,* should be: I give you bones and toys for you to chew on. I like it when you leave my things alone, and chew only on your bones and toys.

How can I entice my pet to leave something alone that she's very interested in?

Do you have children? Have you ever tried to tell them to stop watching TV or stop playing a game when they're totally engrossed in it? What happened? Did they pay attention to you the first time around, or did you have to repeat yourself several times? It's just the same when you're asking your pets to stop doing something you don't want them to do. You must get their attention, and you may have to explain things more than once.

For instance, a lot of dogs pick up special smells during their walks and many want to try out what they find by sampling it, or gobbling it all down. They'll eat anything and everything, including poop that has been left behind from other dogs or cats. Of course, you're concerned and you want them to stop that behavior because it's in their best interest to do so. But how do you go about it?

I sometimes tell them that if they eat what's on the ground, they're going to feel so sick and their tummies will hurt so much that they may want to hide and not eat at all! I may show them a picture where they're throwing up after eating the wrong thing, or they're curled up in a place away from everyone else because they're feeling such distress in their tummies. Or, I show them a picture of their bowl with delicious food in it, but in the picture, they're turning and walking away from it because they don't even want to eat anymore.

Always remember to connect the bad feelings they may be experiencing with what they ate that they shouldn't have eaten.

I also show them that you, as their parent, are going to be very sad to know there's nothing you can do to help. In this scene, I depict you sitting beside them with a look of concern and sadness on your face. I also send them a feeling of your helplessness.

In some instances, I'll even show them that they may have to go see their veterinarian when they've eaten something during a walk.

This method works well for those animals who don't enjoy a trip to the vet. I actually construct very detailed scenarios for them. I send them a picture of what they might see and hear and feel. I even go so far as to feel my stomach being in pain or feeling as if I have to throw up because of what they ate. I show them a picture of getting into the car and arriving at the veterinary clinic. I show them how we'll be going into the waiting room and then into the examination room. In this kind of scenario, I do as much as I can to let them know how they may feel and what may happen if they eat things they shouldn't eat during their walks.

But what if your pet *enjoys* things she eats during a walk and never seems to feel sick or needs to throw up. You'll then need to create a different picture that says very firmly, "Leave it!"

This may be especially true if your pet had a previous owner. It may be that your pet used to have to fight for her food, or scrounge for anything she could find to satisfy her hunger, even from as far back as puppyhood. Or the previous owner may simply never have tried to stop the behavior.

This will be a more challenging task, but you *will* need to find a picture that works for *your* pet, because words alone may never be sufficient to change her behavior otherwise. And you *will* need to teach her first exactly what you mean by "leave it." Do this by putting her food dish down saying, "Leave it." Wait until she looks up at you, then say, "OK."

Once she's mastered the concept, then when you're out walking, send her a picture that says, "Leave it on the ground! Keep walking."

Show her in your picture that she's turning away from whatever's on the ground and leaving it alone. See her keeping her mouth closed and walking away from whatever it is. Tell her you like it very much when she leaves what she finds on the ground. Remember to make each picture and statement convey to her the positive thing you want her to do. (Avoid saying things like, "Don't eat that!")

You may want to add a picture saying that if she does leave it alone, she'll receive something good, and then have a treat ready to immediately reward her with, though it would be much better if she learns to simply respond to the idea of "leave it" without any reward, other than praise, because you may not always have treats handy.

Of course, sending a picture to your pet the first time is only half of it. During your walks, you must continue with the picture in your mind while at the same time reminding your pet out loud: "Remember how much your tummy will hurt if you pick that up." Or, "Leave it! Keep your mouth closed. Keep your mouth empty. Keep walking." You need to reinforce your mind pictures with the actual verbal command, just like you would with a child.

Because our dogs live in the moment, many times they simply forget what you said a few hours ago and they'll need to be reminded, especially at the moment of temptation. This is only in the beginning until they get your picture loud and clear.

I remember when my dog, Princess, was about five years old. She's a little Shih-Tzu and has always been especially lively. She loves her walks so much that she often runs a little ahead of us, especially when the rest of us are moving too leisurely for her active pace. She's very friendly, so she'll walk right up to grownups and children alike to be petted. And she loves other dogs, big or small. It doesn't matter to her; they're all friends.

One day while walking toward the house, and barely twenty feet from her own front door, Princess saw a Golden Retriever. He was on a leash, crossing the street with his Dad. She decided she wanted to go and say hello. I was so scared about the possible dangers she might encounter in crossing the street that I started yelling at her in a panic.

Suddenly, realizing she wasn't listening to me at all, I threw my keys in her general direction, but not directly at her. She stopped as if she had brakes on the bottoms of her paws and immediately looked at me and said, "Oops, I forgot, I'm not supposed to cross the street." She's now thirteen years old and has never done that again.

This is a good example that shows that sometimes our pets will need to have a behavior corrected or reinforced once in awhile.

What if I'm trying to get my dog or cat to be friendly towards others, or to do something that goes against her natural instincts or her desires?

This requires a lot of trust on the part of your pet. She absolutely has to know that your *actions* will support her, and that you *will* take care of any situation that might arise, in a way that's to her liking. If she's not sure that you'll do this for her, she won't be able to trust you.

That means you can *tell* her until you're blue in the face that the other dog won't hurt her, but she won't be able to trust you until you've done two things. You must make it absolutely clear to her that you're in control and keeping her safe, AND, through the pictures you send her, that you know and trust the other dog.

Again, it takes more than just communication; it takes action on your part. Then it's up to the other dog to prove to your pet that the two of them *can* get along peacefully.

The same applies to cats who hide under a bed when they see a stranger in their home, especially if it's someone they don't seem to like, or children whom they don't trust. Communicating to your pet that that particular human is ok is only half the work. The *stranger* then has to prove to your pet that he or she can be trusted.

Finally, how do I get across to my pet that I'm leaving for the day, the night or the weekend?

Here's where your pictures become very important. I often tell my clients to daydream. Make up a mini-movie where you're going to leave home for the day. Picture clearly how the lighting changes from bright to dusk to dark as the hours pass. Look at the window through your pet's eyes, and in your mini-movie, show them how it will look outside when you come back that same day. Also tell them what's going to happen when you return: that you'll go for a walk together, you'll feed them, or, simply, you'll hug and kiss them and tell them how much you've missed them.

If you're going to be spending the night away, extend the mini-movie to show them that it will be dark all night but after it's daylight again, or sunset of the next day, you'll be back home. Also tell them, with a picture as above, what to expect when you come back.

If you're going on a short vacation, do a series of light and dark pictures for every single day you'll be gone and count it out for them. Tell them that you'll send them more pictures from wherever you are to let them know you're thinking about them.

If you're going to be gone for several weeks, you can shorten the process. Pick a day of the week on which you usually do something special together, like a Saturday or Sunday. Tell your pet, with a picture, how many of those special activity days will pass before you return. When it's almost time for you to come home, then you can once again send pictures showing individual days and nights passing so they'll understand that you'll be coming home soon.

It's also important to let them know who will be coming in to feed them or walk them, or simply spend a little time with them, whether they're staying at home or being boarded at a kennel.

They also need to know about any other changes that might happen while you're away. Will someone be taking them to the vet or the groomer? Will they be riding in a different car? Will they spend some time at doggie day care, or at someone else's house? Will they be in a crate, or a cage, or in a dog run at a boarding facility? They have a great capacity for understanding our pictures, our thoughts and our intentions, but we need to be clear in communicating these things to them.

If your pet is particularly sensitive about having you be away, you may want to ask a professional animal communicator to send messages to your pet on your behalf while you're gone. But that doesn't mean that you should stop trying to send messages yourself.

Recently when I was telling a pet that her Mom would be home soon, probably in about two days, she very matter-of-factly told me, "I know. Mom's been talking to me. She can't wait to get back because she misses me, and she misses our big bed."

Later, the client told me that one evening, toward the end of her stay, as she was turning down the bed, she thought about how very small it was compared with her own bed at home. In an off-handed way, in her mind, she immediately said to her pet, "This twin size bed is so small that there isn't even enough room in it for both of us. I hope I'll be home in another couple of days so I can sleep in my own big bed and snuggle with you again, because I've missed you so much during the past two weeks."

The client didn't know whether her pet was actually receiving her messages or not because she didn't have enough quiet time to stop and listen for a response, but her experience clearly shows that it's always worth trying to communicate with your pet, even if the communication is one-sided.

Some closing thoughts

Your pets are always able to receive your pictures since this is their language. It's we who have to make a special effort to change our form of communication into pictures when we're trying to get our point across to them.

Telepathy is like anything else in life. It's a gift or talent that you're born with, but in order to be good at it, you'll need to practice it every day. With practice, you'll soon find that you have your own style and your own way of seeing, hearing, smelling, sensing and feeling the answers to all of your questions.

You may even feel called, as I did, to help not only your own pet, but also as many other animals as possible. Remember that if this is going to be your Life Assignment, you may just be taking your first steps. You might even tend to think you'll never succeed. But don't give in to the temptation to give up quickly if at first you don't see results.

Practice gently and quietly, with peace and serenity, over and over again. Release any sense of pressure or stress to try to "get it" after a certain number of tries.

Practice just being quiet, just being in the moment, just letting go of thoughts, just seeing your pet in your mind's eye. If you do only this much every day for a few minutes, one day you'll become gently aware that you're seeing, hearing, feeling or just knowing something that's definitely a message from your pet.

Whether it's your Life Assignment, or you just want to have a closer relationship with your own beloved pet, it's an immensely rewarding feeling when you know you're able to bridge the communication gap between species.

Chapter 4

Communicating With Your Pets About Health Issues

Once you've learned about intuition, meditation, and how to talk with your pets about everyday activities, there may be times when you'll want to ask your pet to describe how he or she feels. You may want to ask questions like: Are you in pain? Where does it hurt? How do you feel after you take the medicine? Is there something that will make you more comfortable? How can I help you? Or your Life Assignment, like mine, may lead you to become an animal communicator and medical intuitive so that you can help many animals.

*Please keep very clearly in mind that this chapter is **NOT** teaching you to diagnose medical conditions. You will, instead, be learning how to **feel** what the animal feels so that you can communicate that information to your own veterinarian, or to another pet parent, who can share it with his or her veterinarian. Only a veterinarian is qualified to accurately diagnose and treat the pet accordingly. Never, ever, identify yourself as a pet diagnostician unless you have a veterinary degree from an accredited veterinary school. Your role is to be an intermediary, to put into people language what a pet is feeling, to be an animal communicator.*

When the time comes that you need to communicate with an animal about his or her health, begin as usual with meditation, but next, always remember to take an important intermediate step *before* you ask the pet how he or she feels.

After you've become very relaxed during your meditation, *first* clearly identify exactly what your *own* body is feeling. Take a complete inventory of yourself to check out your own aches, pains or other discomforts. Even the most minute of details needs to be taken into account here because you don't want to confuse *your* bodily aches with those that will be coming from your animal companion when you begin scanning her body for *her* feelings.

Once you know how *you* feel, call your pet in your mind and heart to come to you. Again, in your mind's eye, observe every detail as your pet approaches you. Notice the expression in the eyes. Are her eyes clear and bright, or clouded and lacking in spirit? Are her ears up or down, and do they move when she walks? Is her tail wagging, happy to see you, or is her tummy almost dragging on the ground. When she's approaching you, is she calm, excited, sad, agitated, moving slowly or quickly, with ease, or in apparent pain? Make sure to see every detail. Remember, your eyes are closed and you're seeing this picture in your mind and heart.

Ask your pet for permission to do a "body scan" so you can look both inside and outside his or her body. Most animals will feel very comfortable sharing this information with you and will remain by your side, comfortable and relaxed. If this isn't the case, then they're not ready for this type of communication at the moment and you shouldn't force the issue. Try again at a later time.

But if they are agreeable, then continue. I like to think of myself as "being" the animal first in order to feel what they feel. I make a conscious effort to "become" the animal. This gives my consciousness a sort of jolt so that I'm totally focused on the body of the animal in question.

Then I start taking inventory of what's going on both inside and outside the animal's body by remembering how I felt before, and how I feel now when I'm experiencing what the animal feels. It doesn't matter where you start. You can concentrate on any area where you're aware of a specific problem, or if you don't have any information, simply start at the top of your pet's head.

If you now feel sensations in your body that you didn't have in that location before, that's what you're looking for. You might, for instance, experience a localized sharp pain, or a headache, ear problems, blurry vision, nausea or any slight change from the way you felt when you checked your own body just a moment before.

Are you getting a headache now? Are your hands numb, or do they hurt? How about your elbow, or your shoulder? Do you feel a pain in your back? Where's the pain located? Is it in the upper back or the lower back? Did you suddenly experience a leg cramp? A ringing in your left ear? Is it hard to swallow? Are you nauseated?

Any of these feelings, *which represent what your pet is feeling,* can be subtle, or they may come in with such force that if, for instance, the feeling is one of nausea, you may very well want to throw up yourself. It all depends on the sensitivity of you as an individual, and it takes practice, a lot of practice, to learn how to control it. Always remember that it's not your feeling, it's your pet's feeling.

On the outside of the body, check your pet's eyes, ears, mouth, teeth, skin, legs, paws, paw pads, genital and rectal areas and tail. Ask questions about each area to help yourself focus more clearly on any feelings you may be receiving.

If the problem is in a leg, you may feel yourself walking "funny" with a limp. Or you might feel a sharp pain in your leg when, as the animal, you're looking up at the bed and thinking about how it would feel if you tried to jump up. Your animal might even send you back an image of wanting a step or ramp next to the bed, which would make it easier for him to go up or down.

You might ask: Does it still hurt when you jump? Do you feel pain when you walk? How does it feel when you go to lie down? And how does it feel when you have to get up after lying down for quite awhile? Is your leg completely healed now?

The subtle feelings you receive in answer to your questions may come through very rapidly as they do in a fast paced conversation. Don't let anything go. If you didn't get it the first time, try asking the same question again. When I'm asking a question, my "picture" keeps rewinding over and over again until I "get it." Then I can move on to the next question.

Once you have "become" your animal and have "traveled" through the outer structure of his or her body by experiencing every inch of it and recognizing the information in your own body, it's time to move to the inside.

Feel the sensations in the animal's throat. Can you feel in your own body how the animal's throat vibrates when your cat meows or purrs, or when your dog barks? Follow the water or the food down the throat through the esophagus. Ask: How does it feel when you swallow? Do you have any difficulty swallowing?

Follow your pet's breath into the lungs. Ask: Do you have any problem when you breathe? Do you feel as if you're getting enough air when you breathe in? Do you feel congested? Do you feel like coughing? If so, what's making you feel like coughing? Are you having any allergies?

Go into your pet's heart. Is it beating at a regular rate or do you hear it skipping? Is it strong or weak?

How is your pet feeling emotionally? Happy, lonely, fearful, content? Ask: Do you feel loved? Do you want some company? If so, do you want it to be a person or another animal? A male or a female? (Remember, these are not *your* personal wishes. They're the feelings of the pet who's talking to you.)

The heart will let you know a lot of information, sometimes more than you bargained for. It's not unusual for me to sometimes start crying at this point because the love that I receive in my own body is so great and so profound that I can only describe it as a spiritual experience. It's a love so pure, so unconditional, so humble, and so immense, that it permeates every cell in my body. Other times, still "being" the animal I'm working with, I might feel a euphoria which I can hardly contain, because the animal is so happy about her family, her home, her work, her humans, her friends.

When you're ready to leave the heart area, continue by going down into the stomach. Ask your pet: How does it feel? Does your stomach feel as if it's in knots? Are you hungry? Thirsty? What foods do you like? Is there any food that you're eating, or medicine you're taking, that upsets your stomach? Is there anything you need to help your tummy feel better? Do you need any supplements or something added to your diet? (Some animals will automatically lick stones, carpet, plastic or people to compensate for some lack in their diets.)

Once more, the information will be subtle. Be prepared to receive it with all of your senses. It could be a color, a smell, or a taste. You could feel a texture, or see some seeds, an herb or a plant. You may see a picture of something materialize in your mind's eye that's exactly what's upsetting your pet, or is what he or she wants or needs.

Next, check the liver, pancreas and spleen, and then look into the bowel area. Ask: Does it feel fine or does it feel stuffed? Are you uncomfortable in any way? Do you have to strain too much when you go poop? Is there anything I can do to help you?

Then check the adrenal glands and kidneys. You might want to ask: Do you feel any pain? Does it burn when you pee? Do you have to pee more than you usually do?

Continue the body scan until you've checked each and every organ of your pet's body, and until you feel you have all of the information the pet needs to convey to you. Use a picture from a reference book to guide you through the various body systems if this will help.

If your pet is taking medication and you want to know how it's affecting her, ask her about the medicine and "feel" the answer. Does she notice any unpleasant feelings after taking the medicine? Is she nauseated or drowsy? Do the unpleasant feelings go away after awhile? Does the medicine relieve the pain or discomfort? Does it make her feel any better?

As you can see, you are both "being" the animal to feel what he or she feels, and asking questions of the animal at the same time. The questions above are a good place to start, but you'll always need to tailor the questions specifically to each individual pet.

Practice and validation

Practicing with animals who don't belong to you will help you develop this listening skill and help you be more objective than you might be when you're working with your own pet.

Also, any information you may receive can be validated by the pet's parent, so that you can confirm that it wasn't information you might have known beforehand, or information you just consciously thought might be right. Validation is very important. We all need it from time to time because it helps us know that we're interpreting the subtle information we're receiving in the right way.

It's wonderful when, during a consultation, someone tells me: "How did you know that!" or "That was going to be one of my questions." To me, these are reassuring validations that the animals are telling their humans what they want them to know, and that the information is something that their humans wanted to know as well.

Aside from experiencing the validation of another person, I also receive validation from the animals themselves. "How?" you may ask. Just by observing their behavior during our conversation. For instance, some dogs may bark when their response to a question from their human is a profound yes or no, and they don't choose to give any other explanation.

Also, I often tell my clients ahead of time that our talk may cause their pet to look as if he or she has fallen asleep. When pets come to see me, it's so relaxing for them to have a "real" conversation and to finally be able to relay to their humans what they've wanted to tell them for such a long time, that they often fall into a trance-like state and look as if they're sleeping. Many times when their humans see them do this, I hear expressions like "I can't believe it!" or "He never does that!"

Countless times the animals have risen from their "nap" and come directly over to me to give me a kiss when we're done.

You, too, may enjoy some of these experiences if you practice, practice, practice. You can't expect the best results unless you do. If you don't practice your gift, whatever it is, you'll never become proficient at it. Even if you were born with a perfectly tuned ear for music and started playing the piano at age three, you'll never become a concert pianist unless you practice continuously. It's the same with our minds. We can "get it" occasionally, as most of us do fairly often with our intuitive thoughts, but we can only become proficient if we do it all the time.

Summary

Let's review the steps for a moment using a simple summary:
- Know that your Higher Self is always guiding you
- Meditate
- Trust your intuition
- Be absolutely honest
- Treat animals with respect when talking with them
- Become the animal
- Ask questions
- Experience all of your senses responding with answers

- Believe in yourself
- Practice, practice, practice

And if you're going to communicate with your animal about health issues, be sure to check your own body first before trying to receive information from your pet.

Talking out loud to your pet

When you're listening to your pet, it's essential to be in a quiet meditative state of mind, but I also want to emphasize the importance of talking to your pets out loud at other times.

They're able to pick up on your feelings, emotions and intentions when you speak to them. If you're speaking from you heart, you'll automatically form pictures in your mind to go along with your words. It's these pictures that they'll "read," and they'll then understand quite clearly what you're trying to tell them.

For example, if your pet is going to have surgery, describe exactly what's going to happen before, during and after the operation.

Tell her:

- Why this operation is necessary
- How she'll feel better once she recovers from it
- Where the incision is going to be
- How much loving care she's going to receive from the doctor and nurses while she's at the hospital
- How they'll give her some medicine to make her sleepy so she won't feel any pain during the surgery
- How they'll give her medicine after the surgery to help her get well and to relieve any discomfort she might feel afterwards
- Anything specific she needs to know about before, during, or after the operation
- How long it may take her to feel normal again
- How long she may have to lie still while she gets better
- How she needs to leave any incision and bandages alone and keep her tongue away from them (avoid telling her what *not* to do; tell her instead how she *should* act)
- What medicines she may need to take afterwards

- How very much you love her and want to help her get well again, and that you'll do everything you can to make her comfortable

Talking to your pet out loud about an upcoming surgery, or about *anything* happening in her life, will help you become better able to communicate with her. You may not experience any direct confirmation that she understood what you said at the moment, but your efforts will be rewarded when you see your pet being more calm and relaxed before surgery, as well as doing much better while she recuperates.

A closing thought

We're all born with gifts, and if communicating with pets is your gift, you should use every possible opportunity to do so. Once you're able to acquire information every time you sit down with a pet, maybe you'll be ready for the next step of becoming a professional animal communicator and medical intuitive. Could this be your Life Assignment?

Whether it is or not, now that you've learned to talk with your pet, especially about health concerns, you're going to want to be able to take appropriate action. In the following chapters, you'll learn about spiritual methods you can use to help heal your pets and find peace for yourself. We'll be discussing practical healing modalities in the next two books.

Chapter 5

Healing with Prayer, Affirmation, Visualization And Intention

Often, when our pets are in distress, or when a veterinarian can't give any further assistance, we feel helpless, despairing and fearful. Usually, we find ourselves giving in to a sense of hopelessness, worry and floods of tears.

But it doesn't have to be that way!

True, if the time has come for a pet to make his or her transition, it's unwise, and even unkind, to keep trying to restore health when that just isn't going to happen. At those times, we must simply provide the most loving and supportive care we can, and be willing to release our pets from any further suffering and distress when it's clear that they're ready to leave their earthly experience.

But in almost all other cases, there's often good reason to feel hopeful that a pet's health *can* be improved because there are so many possible options available to you. All you need to do is set aside the worry, the fears and the tears, and as the title of the book says, *"For Pet's Sake, Do Something!"* That "something" can be done on a practical level, on a spiritual level, or on both levels at the same time.

We're going to begin at the spiritual level by focusing on prayer, affirmations, visualization and intention, because many of these activities will help *you* become more calm and peaceful about your situation, as well as provide benefits for your pet.

Prayer

Prayers are positive thoughts that have energy, and prayer for another is a selfless form of Love. But does prayer actually make a difference?

Research demonstrating the effectiveness of prayer to assist with healing has even become part of a new emphasis in medicine. The scientific community has now begun to acknowledge that a person is *more* than just his or her body.

Disease (dis-ease) in the body is often a sign that healing is not only needed on the physical level, but it's also needed at other levels. It's not the disease alone that needs to be treated. It's the *whole* person who needs to be healed because there's an essential link between body, mind and spirit. This is true not only for people, but also for animals. And prayer is one way to help heal "dis-ease."

The medical community recognizes prayer, in its many forms, as a noetic therapy—a healing influence performed without the use of a drug, a device, or a surgical procedure. In one study of heart patients at a medical center for veterans, the report showed that those patients who were in the prayer and other noetic therapies group had a 25-30% reduction in adverse outcomes (reported in the November, 2001 American Heart Journal).

On a larger scale, in the movie "What the Bleep Do We Know" there's a depiction of an actual experiment that was done in the city of Washington, DC, which also illustrates the power of prayer, especially when many people join together. Four thousand people united in their intention to pray for humanity and to pray that violent crimes in that particular city would stop. Members of city government and the police department didn't hold out much hope that praying would have any significant effect on an entire city. Yet, after 30 days of focused prayer by the group, it was confirmed that violent crimes had decreased by 25%.

If prayer alone can account for a change this measurable, which touched the lives of so many people in a whole city, think about what the prayer of even one person might do to help the well being of another person or animal. And what if family, friends and church members all unite together in prayer for the same intention?

Simply put, prayer helps. If you want to help your pet when he or she is in distress, you can always pray. You can do this at the same time you're using other healing methods. And prayer can be particularly calming in those situations where you don't know what else to do, or there doesn't seem to be anything else you can do.

Prayer focuses your mind and heart, and whenever we're focused, and the chatter of our thoughts is quieted, we're so much better attuned to God, Spirit, All That Is. It may even be in those moments of prayer that you become aware of receiving an inspiration about what you can do at a practical level to help your pet.

Affirmation

Positive thoughts that we repeat over and over again in our minds are often referred to as affirmations. Sometimes they're even considered to be a form of prayer. And thoughts that we repeatedly affirm have very powerful effects on our lives.

For example, on a positive note, an Olympic skier may remind himself many times a day that he *will* complete his run in even less time than a previously set record. And when the time comes, he does it.

On a negative note, a child may tell himself over and over again that he'll never be able to learn how to do something. And he never does. Yet, if someone comes along who builds that child's confidence by changing what he's constantly been saying about himself, that same child not only learns to succeed at the original task, but may even rise to a level of greatness.

From these two examples, it's easy to see how repeating any thought over and over again in our minds, whether it's positive or negative, can make a major difference in how we act. Our thoughts can either help us burst free and overcome seemingly insurmountable obstacles, or they can hold us back so that we restrict ourselves to living only in a world of limitations.

Sometimes, though, when we find ourselves stuck in a life of limitations, we eventually reach the point where we're *finally* ready to make a change. But the only way to accomplish this is to toss out all of our old limited ways of thinking and create a whole new way of can-do thinking.

It means that we have to choose and affirm new thoughts that move us forward, and we'll have to repeat those same thoughts over and over and over and over again until we find ourselves acting accordingly. This is the process of using affirmations.

But for affirmations to have a positive effect, we have to repeatedly state the same thought *only* in a positive way. We also need to affirm the thought as being true *right now*, not just say that we hope it's something that will come about in the future.

We can also use positive affirmations to help our pets. Remember that our animals readily pick up on our emotions, thoughts, feelings and intentions, and they *will* mirror what they perceive in us. For that reason, by using positive affirmations, you can create a road map to recovery for them, and they'll respond in every instance they can, because they want to please you.

So how do I create an affirmation?

Choose every word very carefully. Your affirmation must convey *only* what you want to see happen in your own life, or in your pet's life.

Eliminate *all* words with *any* negative connotation like: "no," "not," "don't," "can't," "won't," "isn't," "sick," "disease," "inflammation," "wound," etc.

Instead say things to your pet like:
- *You're healing very quickly and completely.*
- *Every cell and every organ in your body is functioning exactly as it should so that you are healthy and vibrant.*
- *The cells in your blood are increasing to exactly the right level to restore you to optimum health.*
- *Your heart is pumping efficiently, maintaining a regular rhythm and a steady beat.*
- *Your breathing is normal and easy.*
- *Your skin around the incision is becoming softer and smoother every day.*
- *Your fur is becoming fuller and more beautiful each day.*
- *Your stamina and endurance are increasing every day.*
- *Every function of your body is perfectly harmonious and balanced once again.*

These are only a few examples of affirmations you might use, but you'll notice that they express only the good that you intend to see. They use words that convey only positive action taking place right now.

Once you've developed the affirmations you want to use, you can make them even more effective by combining them with another process called Visualization.

Visualization

When we use visualization, it's a little like daydreaming. In a visualization, you're creating a movie, using all of your senses. You're bringing to life a clearly detailed picture so that you fully experience in your mind the good outcome you're expecting.

Make your picture as vivid, bright, colorful, optimistic and positive as you can, seeing only the *good* that is coming about.

Visualizations and affirmations are powerful tools which can be used in many instances when you want to help your pets -- from calming them down before a road trip, to stopping diarrhea caused by stress, to relieving separation anxiety when you need to leave home, and of course, for helping to heal anything from a simple scratch to recovering from major surgery.

For example, if you're working with a pet who has been through an operation then:

- See the incision healing as you trace it with your fingers, or as you apply any kind of ointment.
- Visualize the incision becoming less and less noticeable and the skin becoming normal in color once again, with a natural sheen and softness, as the inflammation disappears from sight.
- Hear your pet sigh with contentment, or purr with delight, as you stroke him.
- Taste, in your thoughts, the special diet you're giving him to restore his health. Savor the chicken, turkey or meat knowing that, with each nourishing bite, his health is improving.
- Smell the healing aromas you place around him, whether it's a scented candle, incense, an essential oil, a flower remedy or some herbs.

Remember that either visualizations or positive affirmations alone can be very effective, but when they're used together the results can become synergistic.

Intention

Whenever you're using prayer, affirmations or visualizations to assist in healing your pets, you're creating a positive intention. You're remembering to re-align your thoughts with the goodness that Spirit, God, the Universe, intends for all of Its creatures to enjoy.

There are many other modalities that also use positive intention for the purpose of healing. You may recognize them by the names of spiritual healing, nondirected prayer, intentionality, energy healing, non-local healing, distant healing, Reiki, and Therapeutic Touch, to name only a few. We'll talk about some of these in upcoming chapters.

But whatever modality you're using, positive intention is an essential part of the process, whether a pet is present with you, or at a significant distance from you. Positive intention is what brings you into accord with the will of the Universe to bring about your own, or someone else's, highest good.

The potential results of intention, positive or negative, have been demonstrated in a very unique way by scientific researcher, healer, and popular lecturer, Dr. Masaru Emoto. He created a technology in which he took photographs of frozen water crystals, seen through a microscope, to provide us with visual evidence of the effects of intention.

In his book, *The Hidden Messages in Water*, Dr Emoto describes how, in the pictures of water from clear springs, which were exposed to loving words, there are brilliant, complex and colorful snowflake-like patterns. But in the pictures of polluted water, or water exposed to negative thoughts, there are only asymmetrical patterns with dull colors.

As part of his experiment, Dr. Emoto wrote words on pieces of paper and taped them to a clear glass container filled with regular tap water. He then observed what happened. While sitting with the container in front of him, he also spoke the written words out loud, over and over again.

When words like "love" and "thank you," were taped to the glass container and spoken, and the water was then photographed, he observed that the vibrations from writing or saying those words created the beautiful snowflake or crystalline-like forms. But when he taped words to the bottle, and also when he spoke words like "I hate you," "You make me sick," or "You fool," he noted that the pictures showed distorted, frightening and muddied patterns.

This is visual evidence that all of our written thoughts and all of our spoken words send out a specific vibration, and that this vibration has an effect on whatever (or whomever) our thoughts or words connect with. (This is also true for our *unspoken,* but constantly held thoughts.)

What Dr. Emoto's experiment demonstrated is that water has the ability to absorb, hold, and even re-transmit human feelings and emotions. Consider the consequences of his demonstration when you stop to realize that human beings and animals are comprised of approximately 70% water and that the earth is also comprised of about 70% water.

What does that mean when it comes to the effects of *any* positive or negative thought energy that is directed to a person or to the earth? The results of Dr. Emoto's work make it demonstrably clear that the right or wrong type of thought energy can have a profound impact on the quality of our lives, and even on our whole world.

For this reason, Dr. Emoto believes that water is deeply connected to people's individual consciousness, as well as to the collective human consciousness, and that we can heal ourselves, each other, and our planet by consciously expressing thoughts of love and goodwill.

So when you want to help your pets heal, quiet your mind so that your positive intention can become very clear to you, and consider using prayer, affirmations and visualization to convey the benefits of that positive intention to the one you want to help.

Some closing thoughts

When you embark on any method of healing, realize that whichever one you choose, it's a way to channel Love, the most powerful Healer of All. So it's with Love that you should approach every healing. You can do it! Just *practice* meditating, *practice* using your intuition, the little voice that comes directly from your Higher Self, and *practice* using healing techniques. Know that you're doing the very best you can for your animal, and ask the Universe to work with you.

Many times, my clients will tell me that they *tried* to help their pets, but it just didn't work. When I ask them how often they tried to meditate, to listen to their intuition, to communicate with their pets, or to send healing energy to them, they respond that maybe they did it once or twice, but nothing happened.

Once or twice simply isn't enough! You can't usually become proficient at using any new technique just by reading a single book, attending one lecture, or one workshop, or trying something only once or twice. You must be patient and gentle with yourself. And you must be committed to taking all the time you need to learn a new skill in order to help your pet.

If you're under too much stress to successfully use any of the methods mentioned above, there are always people available who are willing to help you. Don't hesitate to reach out to a prayer group, an animal communicator, or anyone you know who can help you accelerate your pet's healing.

I sincerely hope that the suggestions in this chapter and in the chapters that follow will provide you with the kind of help you need, so that you'll no longer feel helpless or hopeless when you're faced with the serious illness of one of your pets.

Chapter 6

Life Force Energy, Reiki, Cosmic Energy And Remote Healing

In this chapter, I'll introduce you to three other highly effective spiritual healing modalities. You'll need the help of an experienced professional for at least one of them, but with study and the right preparation, you, too, can learn how to use all of them yourself.

In order to understand these three healing modalities more easily, we'll first delve into the wisdom of the ages to learn about Life Force Energy. We'll also briefly explore our ideal form, the importance of energy vibration, how imbalance and disease actually begin with a strongly held thought or feeling, and what healing is really all about.

Once you understand the importance of these concepts, then we'll talk about the healing methods of Reiki, Cosmic Energy and Remote Healing.

Understanding Life Force Energy

Thousands of years ago, Chinese Taoists, believed in an eternal power that moves the universe. Similarly, according to ancient writings from esoteric Buddhism, there's a belief in a force, like a breath of Energy, which permeates the Universe, connecting everyone and everything.

This Life Force Energy is called Ch'i by the Chinese, Qi by the Japanese, and Prana by the Hindus. These are simply different names to describe the very same Life Force Energy, which in Western culture, we call the Universe, Spirit, God, the Source of Our Being, or All That Is.

For centuries, all of these ancient cultures have recognized and studied this Life Force Energy, and they've each developed their own techniques for using it to heal body, mind and spirit.

Human beings and animals are also powered by the same source of energy—the Life Force or Ch'i. It constantly envelops us and travels throughout our bodies like an endless fountain that bathes us in its infinite beauty.

It's the Life Force Energy that we use for healing, and the one we always have protectively around us and within us. It's in constant motion and even seems to be overflowing from our crown chakra at the top of our heads, becoming like a fountain of light, which in the East is known as the "Flowering Lotus," because it resembles one.

It's the part of us that is always connected to the Source of our Being. Though most people go through life unaware of this tremendous energy, those who have learned to be attuned to it, and to use its healing power, experience a special joy.

Each of our lives follows a natural cycle of growth and fading, of yin and yang. Because the yin and yang are immune from the restrictions of time, space, and even any material manifestation of existence, they're able to move freely without any external limitation.

It's the Life Force Energy, or Ch'i, which surrounds our auras and permeates our bodies, which is constantly keeping a balance between the positive and the negative, between the yin and the yang.

The way Ch'i is either freely expressed or blocked in an individual person, or in an animal, has a profound effect on his or her mental and physical condition. When, as human beings, we're out of balance with our Source Energy, Ch'i, we often become aware of experiencing either physical or emotional disease. Bringing ourselves into alignment again can be accomplished in many ways, as the information in this chapter will show. The same is true for our animals.

The perfection of our ideal form

One way to restore balance in our lives requires understanding the perfection of our being. We each have an ideal form. It's the highest and clearest expression of who we are. When one or more negative thoughts or feelings cause a deviation from the perfection of this ideal form, that's when we experience pain or disease, either emotionally or in our physical bodies. This is true for both people and for animals. But if we set aside any thoughts about the problems which are affecting us, and instead hold clearly in mind the image of the perfection of our being, we can then effectively bring about changes not only emotionally, but also in our physical bodies.

Understanding energy vibration

Still another way to heal the imbalance of pain and disease in our lives, or in the lives of our animals, is to understand the concept of energy vibration. Every person, animal and living organism has a vibration unique to itself. This vibration is around us at all times, but we need to learn to pay attention to it. It gives us that sense that something just isn't right, allowing us time to correct an imbalance before it gets any worse. It also helps us to know how others are feeling, either empathetically or empathically.

How imbalances and disease start with a thought

Evidence from many sources, some dating back to the time of Aristotle, supports the idea of an emotional or mental subconscious link to physical illnesses, accidents and circumstances. Any psychologist or psychotherapist will also confirm this connection.

In the case of emotional disturbances, we may appear to be physically sick. But to be healed, all we really need to do is to repair an imbalance, whether that means correcting a phobia, releasing an early experience, or recognizing and releasing a feeling we've simply *assumed* to be true.

Any diseases or discomforts that manifest visibly in the body may, in fact, stem initially from certain negative thoughts or feelings we're holding onto, either consciously or unconsciously. So, if all disease essentially starts with a strongly held thought in the mind before it ever manifests in the body, is it possible for conscious, thinking human beings to program themselves to believe that they're sick, or to believe that they're well? Much of the evidence we now have about curing cancer shows that this is entirely possible.

Understanding imbalances and diseases in animals

But what about our animals? Do they also program themselves into sickness or health?

Animals often act as mirrors of what's happening to us in our own lives. With their uncanny wisdom, they seem to know exactly when they should bring it to our attention that we need to take a closer look at what's really going on with ourselves physically or emotionally. They may even start acting just like we do by having the same aches and pains, moping around, or seeming unusually sad.

Or, when they *choose* to take on the same sickness or emotions we're experiencing, they may think that if they just take our problems on themselves, then that will make *us* be all right once again.

When we begin to experience healing within ourselves, our animals may then start feeling and acting better on their own, though sometimes they need to be told very specifically that it's now ok for them to be well again. The stories in the chapter about spiritual healing in my second book, *Pets Have Feelings, Too!* show this very clearly.

Other times, animals contract diseases of their own as we've also seen in case studies in various chapters in the same book. These diseases may start with an emotional imbalance, a confused memory, or a known fear, and they can be healed by listening to an animal express his or her feelings, as well as by using some alternative spiritual and/or practical healing methods.

When our animals are sick with something like an upset stomach, or they're refusing to eat, or they're recuperating from surgery, it means their vibration is out of alignment with their ideal form. We can, and should, think about using alternative spiritual and practical healing methods to help restore the proper balance in their vibrational level. These treatments can be used alone, if the condition doesn't require medical help, or together with medical intervention, whenever that's necessary.

Healing

So what is healing, and which of the many different methods should you use?

The widely used meaning of the word *healing* most often refers to the relief of symptoms, even when the cause of the problem is not completely corrected. But *true healing* means a return to *wholeness*. Healing, then, means bringing our physical form into closer alignment with our ideal form so that, once again, we're whole, complete, balanced and harmonious.

There are many spiritually based ways to heal an imbalance in a person or animal's energy field or vibration. We'll look at three of them which you may especially want to consider using: Reiki, Cosmic Healing, and Remote Healing.

In all three modalities, either you, or a practitioner, directs and balances the flow of the Life Force Energy for the client or the animal. Some other forms of healing using Ch'i energy, which you may want to research on your own, are Ch'i Gong, Pranic Healing, Quantum Touch, Cellular Repatterning, Toning, Polarity Balancing and T-Touch. They all use the one and only Life Force Energy. Only the technique is different.

Reiki

One of the most recognized forms of alternative healing is Reiki (ray-kee), a Japanese word meaning Universal Life Force Energy. This is the energy that's always around us and within us.

Reiki is a way of directing and applying the Universal Life Force Energy to promote good health, healing, balance and wholeness. Treatment with this technique is useful both for restoring balance, and for preventing imbalance. Reiki energy also helps the body maintain a state of well-being once any imbalances have been corrected.

Practitioners must first learn to become attuned to the Reiki energy, and then they learn to let it flow freely through them. They can use it to treat themselves, other people, animals or life situations.

There are three levels of Reiki. Each of them requires a different level of attunement, and each level of attunement enables a person to more effectively let the Universal Life Force Energy flow through him or her.

The attunements are generally given only in a class conducted by a Reiki Master, someone who has been attuned to Reiki III. A Reiki attunement is the ceremony through which a Reiki Master passes on to the student the ability to easily become aware of and focus the Reiki energy.

Reiki energy is *not* the practitioner's personal energy. It's Universal Life Force Energy, or God Energy, which is unlimited, which is always available, and which simply flows through the practitioner to the recipient.

The energy begins flowing when the practitioner very lightly places his or her hands upon the person or animal to be healed, with the intention for healing to occur. The energy knows where to go and what to do, and manages its own flow within the recipient.

The recipient draws through the practitioner exactly the amount of healing energy he or she needs. All of this happens without any direct mental intervention by the person doing the Reiki treatment. The practitioner's role is only to be a clear conduit through which the Life Force Energy flows, and to watch for and be attuned to signs about where to place the hands next.

A Reiki treatment can also be given remotely to someone at a distance who wants to receive the healing energy in this way. For this purpose, there are several symbols that need to be memorized to help the practitioner focus the energy.

For in-person treatments, a set of progressive hand positions are traditionally taught which give good coverage over the recipient's entire body. These positions are a starting point from which the practitioner should work, though it's important for the person doing a treatment to intuitively place his or her hands wherever the energy seems to be most needed.

Reiki is easily learned, very simple to use, and beneficial for all, including our pets. But before being able to practice the healing art of Reiki, one does need to study, and receive the proper attunements to become a Level I or a Level II Reiki practitioner, or a Level III Reiki Master.

Cosmic Healing

The second healing modality I want to share with you is the one I've practiced for many years. I was using it to help people long before I understood that I could also use it to help pets.

When I studied with Master Tam Nguyen, he taught a particular healing technique, which he called Cosmic Healing. Like Reiki, this is also the process of applying the Life Force Energy to heal ourselves, others, or our pets—physically, mentally and spiritually. Both of these ancient forms of healing are simply a means to channel Love, which is the only energy that heals.

Cosmic Healing, which is derived from Tantric teachings, is a heart-centered technique in which the energy flows through the hands of a practitioner, as it does in Reiki. Master Tam always stressed, however, that it's important for us to remember that we're only the conduits, and that we must never think of ourselves as being the healer. One of the benefits of being the conduit, however, is that the healing energy you're sending to the recipient, also permeates your own body and soul, as it does in Reiki.

In many forms of energy healing, the practitioner generally places his or her hands directly on the client, but in Cosmic Healing, touch is not necessary. However, while we don't usually use any physical contact, we may on occasion use the hands-on technique whenever the Life Force Energy guides us as it's flowing through us.

And just as there are certain symbols used in Reiki, there are also symbols used in Cosmic Healing. These symbols are given by a Master Teacher to those who have studied and practiced Cosmic Healing for a long time. They simply help a practitioner to better focus his or her attention on the specific type of healing which needs to be accomplished.

But you may also use the basic technique of Cosmic Healing, even if you haven't spent many years studying it. Once you've learned to quiet your mind through the use of meditation, to be attuned to the flow of the Life Force Energy which is always all around you, and to have the intention of helping another person or pet to heal, you may then direct this healing energy to anyone who wants your help.

Cosmic Healing for animals

When doing Cosmic Healing on animals, the session takes much less time that it does on a person. For example, if a healing session takes half an hour for a person, it may take only about fifteen minutes for a dog, and probably only about five minutes for a cat. This is because our animals are so sensitive to *all* energy vibrations.

What steps should you take when you want to use Cosmic Healing on animals?

First, encourage the animal to lie down comfortably beside you. I usually prefer to sit next to him on the floor. Some people also choose to put on soft background music, light candles, or burn incense. All these are optional.

The most important thing is your state of mind and your healing intention. You need to be relaxed enough to be totally in the moment, and to focus on the fact that you're the conduit of the healing energy.

Clear your mind of distractions such as "to do lists." Close your eyes and focus on your breathing for a moment. Relax by inhaling slowly through your nose to the count of four in a long, deep breath. Hold the air in your lungs for a count of at least four or longer, and then move the air from your lungs to your stomach and hold it there for another count of four. Now release your breath slowly, slowly, slowly through your slightly open mouth.

As you exhale, your shoulders should sag, your ribs should close in, and your abdomen should push up to squeeze as much stale air as possible from your lungs. You want to get rid of stale air and replace it with fresh, so that you'll be a more effective conduit for the energy to flow through. Do this breathing exercise three times.

If your mind wanders, gently return to your meditation by focusing on your breathing again. Know that you *will* be able to remember everything you need to do when you return to the level of everyday awareness.

When your mind and breathing are quiet and you're ready to receive the healing energy, keep your eyes closed and hold your hands in front of your chest with your palms up. This position should look as if you're asking the question, "Why?" It's essential to pause at this point until you experience some sensation in the palms of your hands. It will usually be a warm tingly or prickly feeling.

The elements in the picture below help to visually illustrate this experience. The light energy you're receiving is represented by the straight centerline of light, as well as by the light lines that come in at a slight angle. The dots of light represent the prickling sensations, while the aura between the dots and the hand symbolizes harnessing the energy in your palms, along with representing what could be a sensation of heat or coolness in your hands. When you feel any of these sensations, you're ready to start sending the healing energy to your pet.

(This picture was actually designed to show the projection of Pranic healing energy, but it's also the most accurate depiction I've found to provide a clear illustration of what it's like to receive the same Universal spiritual energy for Cosmic Healing.)

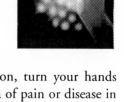

Once you've become aware of this sensation, turn your hands face down and rest them gently above the area of pain or disease in your animal's body. If you're not sure where the pain is, start at the head and work slowly down to the tail.

You have two options for where to place your hands: you can either hold your hands one inch above the body, or touch the animal gently, by barely placing your hands on his or her physical body. I generally use a very light hands-on touch for dogs because they may be a little more relaxed throughout the treatment. However, I prefer the hands-above technique for cats since they're so highly sensitive and usually won't stay around for very long when being touched directly.

While your hands are either touching the animal or gently floating above his body, be aware of your healing intention. Remember that the healing light of Spirit that surrounds you and fills your body is flowing through the palms of your hands into the body of the animal you're treating.

Feel the tingling sensation as the light energy flows effortlessly from your hands into his body. Imagine how this light spreads throughout the animal's body and fills him up from the inside out. Picture this vividly. See it, feel it, believe it.

Hold your hands in each location for several minutes at a time. Follow your intuition and don't intellectualize your movements. Instead, let your intuition and any changing sensations in your palms guide you about when to move your hands into the next position.

You may become aware that your hands feel warmer or colder, but there's always a change, which you'll recognize. Usually a warmer sensation means that the energy is flowing strongly to the location. A cooler sensation may mean it's time to shift your hands to a different location on the animal's body.

When the sensation in your hands lessens noticeably, you can then move them to a different location and continue the treatment, or if the treatment needs to be done only for a single location on the body, simply discontinue sending healing energy after you've treated that specific area.

Since your hands are already flowing with this wonderful loving energy, *you* can take advantage of it, too. When you're finished with your animal friend, say thank you to the Universe, and then place your hands on your own face, or over your own heart, or anywhere you may need the benefit of this loving energy. Inhale deeply, and welcome any healing that's now taking place within you.

You'll learn to recognize when it's time to release the healing energy, either because you'll know it intuitively, or because your pet will let you know. Sometimes when pets have had enough, they'll just get up and walk away. Other times, they leave, only to come back for more later on. You can initiate treatment again at a later time if the pet seems to want to receive the energy again.

When you don't know exactly what ails an animal, there's another technique you can use. When you sense that the energy is flowing, simply cup the pet's face in your hands and look into his eyes. At this time, send love from your heart directly to his heart, while telling him how much he means to you. Tell him you're sending him the healing light of the Universe because you want him to be whole again. During these moments, your heart and mind should be filled with love, peace, joy, compassion, forgiveness, and acceptance. Visualize the healing light flowing freely and lovingly to the animal.

You may see some changes in your pet soon after a treatment, but possibly several sessions will be required. Once again, remember that to be successful, practice is essential. You must always have a quiet mind and a sense of attunement with the Divine to practice Cosmic Healing.

Remote Healing

What do you do when you want to send healing to a person or to a pet who can't be present with you?

In the chapter on Spiritual Healing in *Pets Have Feelings, Too!*, you may have read the story about Thomas and Casey which touched on the idea of remote or absent healing. Whether you're a novice or an advanced healer, a believer or a skeptic, you can easily learn to practice this healing technique. Why? Because it's so easy to send loving healing energy to any other being, or even to a situation!

It's the experience of allowing Universal Love to flow *through* you. It's not you, or your own energy, doing the healing. It's the energy coming directly from the Source of your Being that heals. It's where the experience of Love is directed *through* a person, but is not *from* the person herself. The love and healing are coming directly from God, Spirit, the Life Force Energy. Some people call this the channeling of healing energy. Others call it prayer.

Remote healing, and also in-person healing, both start with the process of *attunement*, or focusing your attention on the Universal Light or Source. In this state of spiritual attunement or meditation, you could say that we use "healing concentration" to send this flow of Love. The main consideration for using this gift is to believe in a strong link between you and Spirit (God). To regularly practice absent healing, you must *regularly* practice being in a state of uplifted consciousness and spiritual attunement. This is true whether you're a beginner or an experienced healer.

Everyone can do this. To send remote healing, all you need to do is:

1.   become quiet in mind and body; and
2.   concentrate on letting healing energy flow through you into the body of whomever you're trying to help.

If you're aware of what disease you're dealing with, you can concentrate the healing as a beam of light directed at the affected area, and then enlarge it to cover the whole body. Visualize it as a beam of light coming from the heavens, with a white and shimmering substance permeating the person or animal's being.

See it, feel it, and send it, knowing that it's having an effect immediately. If you don't know what kind of disease or injury needs to be treated, then send the beam of light directly from your heart center to the animal's heart center, and let its body decide how best to use the energy.

There's no set format you need to follow for doing remote, or absent, healing. It can be done at any time, though if you're doing it regularly, it's often a good idea to do it everyday at the same time and in the same location. Pick a quiet time and place where interruptions can be avoided. It shouldn't take you any more than a few minutes.

How do you spiritually locate the person or pet to whom you want to send remote healing?

If you're helping someone you don't know well, sometimes you'll need more information than just a name. In general, the more specifically you identify the recipient, the more effectively you can focus the energy to promote recovery and well-being. That's why I often ask for a photo, the animal's name, age, breed, sex and the city he or she lives in. I want to be able to find my remote target when I talk to the heavens. If you tell me only that your dog's name is Fluffy and she's white, it may take me a little longer to find the Fluffy who belongs to you.

Since there are thousands of Rovers, Princesses, Samantha's and Fluffy's out there, I have, on occasion, linked common animal names with the names of their owners to help me locate the right one. For instance, I would ask Spirit to please send healing energy, through me, to the little two-year-old Pekingese, in a specific city, who's fighting for his life, who belongs to Mark and Cindy.

As part of my Life Assignment, I've always sent remote healing to the animals I "talk" to. Yet, knowing that the Universe has its own plan for each of us, including our animals, and knowing that we all have the ability to choose, I always end my healing request with the words: For the Highest Good of All!

Some closing thoughts

How would you know if you're not supposed to do a healing?

It takes a little practice, and you must look and listen for an indication. Some people see a red or a green light in their mind's eye; others get a certain feeling in their heart center, yet others hear an actual "no" in their head. The novice might not get any information until he or she has practiced for some time, but for the advanced student, this information will quickly become clear.

Even if you sense that you're not supposed to send the energy for the purpose of healing, you always can, and should, send *loving* energy to that person or pet.

What if healing doesn't occur?

If a healing doesn't occur, it may mean that it's not meant to be part of the recipient's life plan. Possibly the person or animal has already fulfilled its purpose in this lifetime, or it no longer has the will to live, and we must honor that.

When healing doesn't take place, it doesn't mean that you've failed, or that you aren't able to let the healing energy flow through you. On these occasions, we must accept the fact that healing doesn't always occur, then bless the situation, and let it go. The love you send will always be received, whether it results in a healing or not. And Spirit will always see to it that whatever happens is for the highest good of everyone concerned.

Chapter 7

Auras

There are two spiritual, or energetic, components of the *essence* of our being. They're called Auras and Chakras, and you'll soon see how they're each an integral part of the healing process, both for people *and* for animals.

In this chapter about Auras, we'll explore some basic information about what they are, how we're aware of them in everyday living, how they relate to a person or to an animal's state of health, and how to heal them.

Most people, who have heard *something* about auras, often believe they only have one. But this isn't so! Even though we sometimes speak about it *as if* we only have one aura, in fact, every living being has at least four. And another protective layer of light, or Universal Life Force Energy—often called Ch'i energy— surrounds those four main auras.

However, as you're reading this chapter, there *will* be a few times when you'll notice we simply say "the aura." If you see the word used this way, try to picture in your mind the combination of all four individual auras surrounded by the light of the protective layer of Ch'i energy.

Introduction to auras

Most people usually believe that the only *body* they have is a physical body. This definitely isn't so!

A person or an animal's physical form is *always* surrounded by *at least four energy bodies, which we call auras.* These combined energy bodies extend out from our physical form by a few inches to as much as five feet or more in all directions. *Their purpose is to guide and direct our physical bodies.*

All of our auras are also protected, infused and powered by an egg shaped layer of light that we sometimes call Ch'i energy. In much the same way that a ray of light from the sun is never separated from its source, we're never separated from our Source either, so this Universal Life Force Energy, or Ch'i, is *always* present around us to love, guide and nurture us. Though we may not be conscious of It, we live and move and have our being in It at all times.

We may not easily be able to see the four main auras or Ch'i energy, but all of us are frequently more aware of them, at least intuitively, than we ever consciously realize.

When we're physically close to someone else, the auras of that person or animal intermingle with ours. If it's someone we love, this intermingling is a pleasant experience. But if we're subconsciously aware of an unpleasant feeling, it's usually because there's something about the auras, or the vibrational energy level, of the other person or animal that isn't compatible with ours, or may even be detrimental to us.

The four main auras (which I'll describe in more detail below) are in constant motion, and tell us important things we need to know about ourselves, or about the animal or person we're trying to help.

Each one of the individual auras projects what a person or an animal is feeling in the form of changing colors, or projectiles of light. Auras are not always uniform or round with a single color. In the majority of cases, they have breaks, tears, ragged sections, swirls, patterns and protrusions where a specific illness or imbalance is showing up.

The healthier one is, the stronger and more beautiful their auras will be. As one becomes more spiritual, the light of the different auras that emanate from around the physical body will become even more intense and vibrant. However, when a person or an animal is in poor health, their auras will appear to be much less vibrant and seem to be thinner and closer to the body.

Sometimes when we're experiencing feelings of anger, the colors of the auras may even seem to "explode" around us. For example, a person or an animal could initially be engulfed in a rainbow of beautiful, peaceful aura colors, but if something causes that person or animal to have an angry reaction, his auras might look, for the moment, as if he's in the middle of a fire pit with bursts of red sparks spewing all around.

Kirlian photography continues to provide visual evidence of aura activity. It's been used for more than 50 years to document the high frequency energy fields of auras, which emanate from all living organisms.

Animals and some people, especially children, are able to perceive auras with their physical eyes. It's even possible to train your own physical eyes to see the shimmering colors of these auras, but most of us only reach that level of awareness when we learn to become much better attuned to our spiritual or intuitive selves.

The auric emanations around the head are the ones most easily detected by other people. They're often seen as a sign of spiritual illumination, and are frequently depicted as halos in works of art. A white halo represents the perfect combination of all the colors of the universe blended in perfect harmony. For this reason, people who're considered illuminated will often be shown in illustrations as having a white halo.

The four auras

The four main layers in a person or animal's auric field are often referred to by several different names: the four energy fields, the four subtle energy bodies, or simply, auras. Every person, every animal, and every living organism has them. Some healers are able to perceive even more than four aura layers, but for our purposes, we'll be talking about only the four main auras.

1) **The Etheric Aura or Etheric Double:** This is the first of the aura energy fields. Generally we can see one to two inches of the etheric aura surrounding the physical body. It's a dense white energy; therefore it's the easiest to see. It follows the exact outline of the physical body and is sometimes called an energy twin of the physical body.

At the moment of sudden or violent death, the etheric double floats away from the physical body. This is the same bodily form that a person is aware of when he has a near death experience and observes himself floating above the scene, for instance, when he's in surgery, or he's appeared to die in an accident. A clairvoyant will be able to see this image in the same detail as it appeared when the person was living.

71

2) **The Emotional Aura:** The second energy field is much less dense than the etheric aura. It stores emotional feelings and displays them in different colors. In animals, the second, or feeling, layer of the aura extends far wider than the boundaries of even the *total* human aura.

We know that emotional pain often leads to physical disease in both people and animals. Most medical healers believe that every disease has an emotional component that must be released for full healing to take place. This release occurs in the emotional aura.

The dog who's been abused suffers from more than just the physical effects of that abuse. Some of his emotional reactions may continue long after he's come to live in a new and caring environment. Even in a safe home, he may be excessively afraid or shy. He may act out with bad behavior, or if he gives up altogether, he may simply languish and die.

By clearing the emotional aura of its negative components (the feelings of being unloved, unwanted, insecure, shy, etc.) the animal can then become rebalanced, and physical disease can be healed (when it has already manifested in the physical body), or it may be avoided altogether (if the problem is corrected soon enough).

3) **The Mental Aura:** The third energy field is related to the mental, or thinking, state of a person or animal's being. Because it's finer and thinner than the emotional aura, it's even more difficult to see. Those who see auras see them as a rainbow of colors, and if they're able to see the mental aura, they usually perceive it as shooting projectiles of light and color.

Animals *do* think, though their perception is different from that of humans. Many of their bad behaviors originate from misguided thoughts and need to be healed at the level of the mental aura.

For instance, an animal who shows fear of water, grass, an inanimate object or a person is associating something he's encountering in the present moment with a previous negative experience. In his mind, everything that is even similar reminds him again of the pain of that original experience. Therefore he associates what's happening right now with a terrible outcome. But we can recondition his feelings by working on his mental aura.

4) **The Spiritual Aura:** The fourth energy field is the finest
and thinnest energy layer and is therefore the hardest to
see. It reflects our spiritual being, and our ability to be in
touch with our Higher Self and with Spirit. An animal's
spiritual aura is similar in size to that of their emotional
aura, although it's much finer.

Pets are as spiritual as people, if not more so. They have a
oneness with earth *and* Spirit that few humans ever experience.
Many cats actually live in this state of being and are readily able to
see and hear things from the spirit world.

Animals may often need healing at the spiritual level for several
reasons.

Sometimes a pet will decide to mimic the same symptoms of
illness or emotional distress that he's observing in his human
companion. He may be trying to act like a reflection of that person.
He's trying to make his friend aware of the fact that the person
needs to do something to improve how the person is feeling. Or, a
pet may even hope that if *he'll* just take the whole illness completely
on himself, then his special person will be freed from it entirely.

After the human companion has recovered, the pet may *still*
continue to manifest symptoms, even though he doesn't actually
have any disease. That's a sign that the pet's healing needs to take
place on the spiritual level. This was illustrated by several pets in
the chapter about spiritual healing in my second book, *Pets Have
Feelings, Too!*

Other times, when there's an imbalance in the spiritual aura, a
pet may need to be made aware of his purpose in life, or he may
need a special job to perform regularly. This is especially true after a
traumatic event, like a debilitating accident or illness, or after the
passing of a close companion.

If animals believe they don't have a purpose in life, or when they
feel there's no place for them, they may choose to die earlier than
they would otherwise. This may also be true for an animal who
remains in close spiritual contact with other pets who have passed
on.

We can help animals overcome many of their spiritual challenges
by healing their spiritual auras. You'll learn how to do this later on
in the chapter.

73

Auras and disease

Auras are part of the *essence* of our being, not part of our physical bodies. It's in our auras that we experience thoughts and feelings. But thoughts and feelings need to find a *visible* manifestation, so whatever we experience in each one of our four auras will eventually be manifested in our physical form.

It helps if we understand that the etheric aura, the one that's closest to our physical bodies, is like a blueprint that creates and maintains our physical form and transmits energy to our bodies.

If a person or an animal is overly stressed, then the effect of those stressful thoughts, which came from the energy of the etheric blueprint, will eventually manifest visibly as a disease in physical form.

Thoughts and feelings that begin in the spiritual, mental or emotional auras also filter downward, to the etheric body, and their effects, too, will eventually manifest visibly in our physical form. If they're positive, we'll enjoy vibrant good health. However, if they're negative, then we'll no doubt experience a temporary or a chronic illness. The same is true for our pets.

In general, diseases which have their origin at the physical (etheric) level are much easier to clear than those which have an emotional, mental or spiritual beginning. However, with effective changes at any level, plus a will to live and a purpose to fulfill, both people and animals can return to a full and healthy life.

It's also true to say that whatever has manifested in our *physical* form can then be observed in our auras. When a disease has manifested visibly in the physical body, after having begun at any one or more of the four energy levels, the *effects* of that disease will then travel *outward* from the physical body and be reflected in one or more of the four auras. Experts who can see auras will be able to use this energetic information to identify where the cause of the disease is located, and possibly even to identify how to correct the imbalance.

With this in mind, it's a little easier to see that treating only the symptoms of a disease won't, by itself, cure the disease. To affect a cure, one must find and correct the original cause. And that cause doesn't lie in the physical body. The cause is going to be found in the energy fields, or auras, that surround the physical body.

It's true that people and animals frequently recover from an illness after their symptoms have been treated, but that's usually because, during the time they were recuperating, subtle changes were taking place in their auras, often nurtured by the loving care they received during that time.

Animals and auras

Animals can also see auras and use the information much more fully than humans can. An animal who sees your auras will immediately sense what kind of a person you are, and decide on the spot if you're a right match for him or her.

I encounter a lot of people who say, with good reason, that they feel as if they're magnets for lost pets who always seem to find a way to their doors. I jokingly tell them, "Just above you, there's an invisible sign in shining bright lights which only pets can see. This is a part of your aura. It reads, 'ALL PETS WELCOME!'"

The accompanying diagram will help you better visualize the four main auras of an animal.

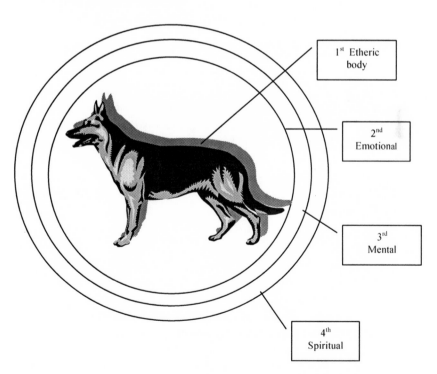

1st Etheric body

2nd Emotional

3rd Mental

4th Spiritual

The colors of the aura

The most common aura colors are red, orange, yellow, green, blue, indigo and gray. Many expressions in our language may even be the result of observations made by people who could actually see the colors of auras. You've no doubt seen cartoons where someone was turning "red with anger." How about hearing someone say she's "green with envy," "in a blue mood," or "in a black fit of temper." Or how about calling someone a "yellow coward" when they're afraid of confrontation. All of these expressions may well reflect the actual colors of an individual's aura in these situations.

Even though there are seven main aura colors, the colors of each aura will vary immensely depending on what a person or animal is feeling, or on what the circumstances are at the moment.

Since the aura is a reflection of constantly changing life energy, the different shades and hues are almost infinite in number. The numerous pastel shades represent thoughts and intentions, as well as the degree of spirituality, while the brighter, bolder colors reflect a person or animal's emotional state.

The following descriptions of aura colors will help you understand the qualities associated with some of the various shades.

Red:
The color red is the easiest one to see. Dull red is a sign of nervous excitation. A red that's muddy or very dark indicates viciousness or a bad temper. The animal manifesting this shade may be unreliable, treacherous, and likely to get into fights. A dull red, or reddish-brown over an organ of the body indicates that a disease may appear shortly, or an illness is going to afflict the body later on unless preventative steps are taken. Red that is flashing or speckled in the area of the jaw indicates a toothache.

Orange:
Shades of orange are often seen around animals who show special consideration for others. They live to serve and often have jobs working as service animals like seeing-eye dogs. A yellow-orange color is a positive sign of self-control and virtuousness. Brownish-orange indicates a lazy dog. When a shade of orange is seen over the

kidneys, it's an indication of possible disease. If there's also a gray blur in it, this may be a sign of kidney stones.

Yellow:

Yellow always denotes good spiritual and moral health. Golden yellow is the sign of a very spiritual nature. All the great saints were depicted with golden halos around their heads. The greater their spirituality the brighter was the glow of golden yellow around them. A more degraded yellow, like that of cheddar cheese, signifies a cowardly nature. Yellow-green around the body may indicate a liver problem. If the color is more brownish-yellow with jagged bands around the head, it could be a sign of mental affliction.

Green:

Green is the color of healing, the color of teaching, and the color of physical growth. A wonderful animal teacher-companion will radiate green with bands of swirling blue, like an electric blue. There may also be narrow bands of golden yellow. Animals with green in their auras are friendly, compassionate and considerate. On the other hand, a more lime green shade indicates a mixture of green with yellow, which could indicate a liver problem.

Blue:

The brighter the blue the healthier the animal is. Pale blue is an indication of shyness while darker blue shows determination and commitment. Certain shades of blue, like smoky blue, also indicate intellectual ability.

Indigo:

Indigo, violet and purple are often perceived as the same color. When seen around the upper part of the body of humans, these colors are an indication that the person may be very spiritual. These colors also indicate a strong connection to spirit in animals. However, pink mixed in with indigo means there may be some kind of spiritual disconnection. When any of these colors are seen around the lower part of the body, it may mean heart trouble or stomach disorders.

Gray:

Gray is a modifier for all colors of the aura. In and of itself it means nothing, but when you see patches of gray in an otherwise colorful area of the body, it could indicate that an organ is in danger of breaking down, or is breaking down, and medical attention should be sought immediately. A dull throbbing headache will have a gray smoky cloud going through the halo, and no matter what color the halo, the gray bands going through it will pulsate in time with the throb of the headache.

Visualizing auras and the light of Ch'i energy

For those who would like a more visual understanding of the four auras, and the Ch'i energy layer, the following may be helpful.

For the purpose of this illustration, imagine that the four auras that encompass the physical body are all rather thin, each being about one inch wide. They're completely surrounded by the light of the Ch'i energy. While this light appears to be an egg shaped layer about two inches wide, which extends beyond the four auras, its light also permeates and infuses the four inches of all the aura layers.

When someone is looking at another person or an animal, all he or she normally *can* see is about six inches of light around the body. For this reason, it appears to most people that there's only a single aura, and that's why it's not uncommon for people to refer to what they see as "the aura." There are very few people, in fact, who can actually see the *separation* between each of the four main individual auras themselves, and between the auras and the Ch'i energy layer.

Why then is it possible for a fair number of people to see the "fire pit" effect if a person is very angry? When this happens, the shooting projectiles of color extend so far out that they become visible all the way to the outer edges of even the two-inch Ch'i layer. This enables people, who can perceive the six inches of light, to observe colors that would otherwise only be visible to someone who can distinguish between each of the four main individual aura layers and the layer of Ch'i energy.

Always keep in mind, though, that the actual width of "the aura" which anyone can see around another person, will depend on the state of physical, mental, emotional and/or spiritual health of the person being observed.

Learning to see auras

When you're first learning to see auras, lighting conditions do make a difference. One method is to position your subject with the sun behind him, whether he's outdoors or in front of a sunny window. You're trying to use backlight so that when you look at the dark outline of your pet, it will be easier to see the light from his auras. If your pet is white, then place him in front of a pastel curtain in front of a sunny window.

Another method is to position your pet in front of a dark cloth or wall. Black is the best choice, but dark purples, violets or browns will also work. The lighting should be indirect, and it's better to use candles for this purpose instead of electricity. However, if you prefer, you may use incandescent lights, but do avoid fluorescent lighting.

Once your pet is positioned, take a few moments to tune out all distractions and center yourself by breathing in and out several times, releasing all worries and tensions in your mind and body. Feel yourself becoming comfortably centered and relaxed.

When you're ready, you shouldn't look directly at your subject. Instead, you'll be *gazing*. Think of it as a very soft look, with your sight slightly shifted to the side of your pet, but not looking directly at him.

Do you remember those 3-D pictures from a few years ago? You had to gaze at them for a while before you were able to experience the depth of what you were looking at. Looking at an aura is similar. Some people even find it helpful to let their eyes slightly cross in order to see an aura more easily. Gradually, you'll begin to see some light around the head and shoulders. You may even be able to observe a soft glow of light just above your pet's back.

You'll need to identify what color or colors you're seeing, but this may be difficult at first because they're usually very soft and subtle. Although you're looking for pastel colors representing the seven colors of the rainbow, you also need to look for any other soft or bold colors you're able to perceive.

Sometimes, the image you see may suddenly appear to be there, but if you try to look for exactly the same image again, it will be gone, or be different, and you can't recapture what you originally saw. Your mind reacts in an instant, like a camera taking a snapshot, while your brain tries to decide what it is that you just saw.

This happens because the energy of the auras is always in constant flux. They may change shape, ripple, or move in wave-like motions. As you're observing them, it's also important to watch for abnormalities like sparks, breaks and shooting lights.

To understand what you're seeing, you need to remain calm and in a heightened state of awareness while making mental notes about what you see. By mastering your ability to be in a state of heightened awareness, you'll be able to perceive information beyond what the physical eyes can see. Remember that you're not only seeing with your physical eyes, but you're also observing with your spiritual vision through your third eye, which is the center of intuition.

Feeling your own aura energy

Even if you never develop the ability to *see* each of the four energy bodies individually, you can still learn how to *feel* the energy coming from those four auras, and from the Ch'i that surrounds them, whether they belong to you or your pet.

To do this, you should practice one or more of the following exercises until you're readily able to recognize the sensations associated with your own auras and Ch'i energy.

While practicing any of the various techniques, once you've begun to experience those sensations, you may then want to place the palms of your hands on your face for a few moments so that you can breathe in the wonderful benefits of the Ch'i energy you're experiencing. Remember, this is the loving Universal Life Force Energy, which is always available to you, and to your pets.

To end an exercise, place the palms of your hands together for a moment, then shake them off, especially if you're going to practice several different exercises in a row.

Exercise 1

Sit or stand with your back straight. Place your hands together as you would in prayer. The tips of your fingers should just barely be touching each other, while the palms of your hands should be farther away as if forming a triangle. Close your eyes and sit meditating (free from conscious thoughts) for at least 15 to 20 minutes. You might not notice anything happening at first, but soon, if you open your eyes, you'll realize that your hands have drifted apart from each other by as much as 2 to 12 inches. The tingling or heat sensation you're feeling between your hands is the combined energy of your four auras and your Ch'i. We also call this your aura energy.

Exercise 2

Sit or stand with your back straight. This time, hold the palms of your hands facing each other about 12 inches apart. Gently move your hands in and out about half an inch at a time. Gradually bring the palms of your hands closer together, continuing the in and out motion, until they're about three to four inches apart. This distance may be more or less, depending on your present state of health and/or spiritual attunement. The sensation you feel in between your palms, which was getting stronger and stronger as you were bringing your hands closer and closer together, is the energy of your aura and Ch'i. You may also feel heat or a tingling sensation. Simply observe what you're feeling, and recognize that you can, in fact, feel your aura energy.

Exercise 3

This exercise will help you sensitize your hands to very subtle feelings. Several times a day, with your eyes closed, blow little puffs of air onto the center of the palm of each hand, one hand at a time. Let yourself be fully aware of whatever you feel. Learning to experience these delicate sensations might be compared, in a way, to the task of learning to read Braille. It's not easy to be sensitive to all of those little Braille dots unless your full attention is placed on the task at hand.

When you're learning to feel energy, you need to practice this type of technique often, until feeling the energy comes automatically to you, just as reading by feeling the dots becomes automatic to someone studying Braille.

Exercise 4

This exercise is yet another way to become sensitive to subtle energy feelings. Place your right thumb in the center of your left palm. With a gentle twisting motion back and forth, use the thumb to activate the energy center in the palm of your hand. Close your eyes and become aware of any subtle changes. Is there a tingling sensation in the palm of your hand? Did you feel a warm or even a hot sensation? When you removed your thumb, did it feel as if your thumb was still touching the palm of your hand, even several minutes after you'd removed it? Repeat the same exercise with your other hand.

Experiencing your pet's aura energy

When you're ready to check your pet's aura (the combination of his four energy bodies and the Universal Life Force Energy, or Ch'i, which surrounds them), always become centered and relaxed first. Then focus your attention toward his physical body. With the palms of your hands facing your pet, move your hands closer and closer to his body until you feel a slight resistance, or a tingling sensation in your hands. This resistance is soft and gentle. It doesn't stop you from moving your hands even closer to your pet's body, but when you do begin to feel it against your hands, you know that you're now beginning to feel your pet's aura.

To reassure yourself about where the aura starts, once you think you feel it, move your hands back a little ways, and then move them forward again toward your pet until you feel the gentle resistance once again.

Use both hands at the same time when you're first learning to feel your pet's aura. Later on, you may be able to use only one hand.

As your hands move around the aura of your pet, ideally you should feel a uniform flow of energy. However, if your pet isn't well, then you need be aware of any anomalies in his energy field. You may sense a warm spot, a cold spot, a tingling sensation, or an empty feeling. Make a mental note of what you experienced, but continue to check every part of his body. You should feel something. If you don't, then stop, and take time to center yourself again. When you're ready to continue, begin again with the palms of your hands facing your pet and start at the top once more.

It's wise to practice this every so often, even when your pet is well. That way you'll learn to recognize how far out his aura normally extends when he's in good health. When your pet is ill, you'll then notice that his aura seems to begin much closer to his body.

Unless you're able to feel your pet's aura right away, go back and do exercises 3 and 4 for five to ten minutes each day for at least two weeks. Be sure to do this before you try to heal the aura.

Healing an aura

Once you've learned to either see or feel your pet's auras, you'll then be ready to help heal imbalances that periodically disrupt your pet's energy field.

In this section, I'd like to share several wonderful and easy-to-learn ways to heal auras. When you do this kind of healing, you're actually cleansing all four auras at the same time, as well as brushing away any negativity which has become stuck anywhere in your pet's energy field.

You don't need to be able to see the individual auras to do this type of healing. You need only to be able to feel your pet's aura energy because you'll be working at the height of your pet's auric field.

Method 1

The technique I like best is the one used in Pranic Healing. First, you'll find the height at which your pet's aura begins; then with a brushing motion in the air from head to tail, you'll sweep away any negative energy from his aura, and shake it off. These are the steps to follow:

Hold your hands about two feet away from your pet. Then with your eyes closed, slowly bring the palms of your hands closer and closer to your pet's body until you begin to feel the energy of his aura. If you then open your eyes, your hands should be somewhere between an inch and a foot away from his body. If his aura energy has been depleted by illness, you'll find that your hands are much closer to your pet, but if he's somewhat healthy your hands will be farther away from him.

Once you know you're feeling the energy of his aura, start at the top of his head and make a single brushing motion all the way from his head to his tail, but without actually touching his physical body. Just let your hands follow the outline of his body at the height of his aura.

When your hands reach the tip of his tail, make believe you're then shaking the negative energy you've collected off into the air, onto the floor, or into some kind of a container. Do this all over his body, from head to tail. Then sweep your hands from his back down the length of each leg to the tips of his paws.

Your intention is to remove from his aura all of the negative energy that's making him sick. It's a little bit like sweeping crumbs away from the table.

Method 2

This next method is one that is used in American Indian culture, or by healers known as Shamans. You'll need some type of a feather. It may have come from a feathered creature like a peacock, an owl, or even a turkey. Because animals are so tuned in to Mother Nature, it's imperative, though, that it come from another living being. It must never be synthetic. First, feel your pet's aura and then make sweeping motions with the feather in the area of his aura, going over his entire body.

Method 3

Light a smudge stick of sage, lavender or sweetgrass. First, feel your pet's aura and then, with the smudge stick, make sweeping motions over his entire body in the area of his aura. Let the aromatic smoke (smudge) cleanse, refresh and revitalize your pet's auric field.

Method 4

Give your pet a healing bath. Put a cup of sea salt, Epsom salts, or baking soda into the bath water, then allow your pet to soak in this solution for five or ten minutes. (Use more or less than a cup, depending on the size and weight of your pet.) If his body is not entirely covered by the water up to his neck, scoop the water over the top of his body using your hands or some type of container.

Method 5

Place your favorite aromatic flowers and sandalwood around your pet's body to act as absorbing agents while repeating a healing mantra.

One meaning of the word "mantra" defines it as a tool to focus one's thoughts. It's the repetition of sounds or words that helps to keep our attention focused so that we can more effectively connect with the healing energy of the Universe.

One of the most familiar mantras in eastern culture is Om Mani Padme Hum. This is a phrase in the ancient Sanskrit language. It's believed that repeating this mantra, silently or out loud, invokes the powerful attention and benefits of the Bodhisattva of Compassion.

But a mantra can also be thought of as a special form of prayer. The mantra you use may be any words or sounds of your choice, possibly a phrase from a favorite prayer, or a healing thought that touch your spirit. It's not the mantra itself that does the healing. It's an individual's faith that helps bring about the beneficial effects from using any mantra.

Additional aura healing modalities

There are many other wonderful tools available to us for soothing and healing the auras of both pets and people. These may include calming music, lighted candles (particularly a white candle which represents healing), quartz crystals (which have excellent healing properties), Australian rain sticks, Tibetan bells, and even spending time in nature with trees, plants and flowers.

The purpose for using all of these helpful tools is to optimize the release of negative energy by clearing, cleansing, and refreshing the aura, especially for a pet who is sick.

A closing thought

Now that you have an appreciation for the importance of auras in relation to healing, for pets as well as for people, you'll learn in the next chapter about chakras and their usefulness in the healing process.

Chapter 8

Chakras

As you learned in the previous chapter, our physical bodies are surrounded by four auras which are powered by Ch'i energy. Chakras, which are considered to be part of the etheric aura, help to distribute Ch'i energy between the etheric body and the physical body. They're depicted in diagrams in a way that shows their close relationship to the nervous and endocrine systems of the physical body.

The word "chakra" means "wheel" in Sanskrit, and the chakras are often seen as spinning wheels of energy. These subtle energy centers are vortices of shifting sounds, colors, and densities which clairvoyants, and others with the ability to see them are able to perceive.

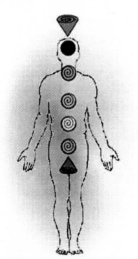

7th - Crown Chakra - Violet

6th - Third Eye Chakra - Indigo

5th - Throat Chakra - Blue

4th - Heart Chakra - Green

3rd - Solar Plexus Chakra - Yellow

2nd - Navel or Sexual - Orange

1st - Root Chakra - Red

When chakras are misaligned, dull, non-responsive, or closed, a person or an animal may show signs of discomfort, or even illness.

It's important at those times to balance all of the chakras in order to bring about a return to health and wholeness.

As you can see in the illustration above, the seven primary chakras in human beings are aligned from the base of the spine to the top of the head. They're identified as: The Root, the Navel, the Solar Plexus, the Heart, the Throat, the Third Eye (or Brow), and the Crown Chakra. Each one corresponds to a specific color.

An animal body also has seven main chakras within its etheric aura. It's through these seven chakras that an animal exchanges essential energy between its auras (the four subtle energy bodies) and its physical body.

An animal's thoughts and feelings, from each of the four subtle energy bodies or auras, filter down through the seven chakras, where they then manifest as certain behaviors, or as states of illness, or of health and well-being in the animal's physical body. (The list of chakra associations at the end of the chapter provides some specific examples of these behaviors and conditions.)

While an animal has seven primary chakras, there are individual variations as to which ones are immediately open and which ones may need to be developed.

The three chakras in animals that are open at birth are the root, solar plexus and crown chakras. At about three months, most pets will have at least five active primary chakras, which now include the navel chakra and the heart chakra. Only a few individual animals actually need to develop the heart chakra. That's because it's already so highly developed in some pets that they're simply "all love" right from the beginning.

Pets operate fully on psychic levels and are totally connected with Spirit. Consequently, in animals, the crown and brow chakras (the middle and higher spiritual layers) usually function as one. Since most animals are already so intimately connected to Spirit, and don't need to evolve spiritually as much as humans do, they don't need to develop one spiritual center before developing the other. We humans, on the other hand, need to be in touch first with our "self" through the third eye or brow chakra, and then in touch with God, Spirit or Higher Self through the crown chakra.

Both human and animal bodies also contain many other subtle energy points, called minor chakras, and in the case of pets, bud chakras. These minor chakras and bud chakras are lesser energy points, but are essential to the vitality of the animal. Animals have up to 21 Minor Chakras and 6 Bud Chakras (4 paw pads, and the bud of skin at the opening of each ear). The bud chakras near the ears are like 9-1-1 emergency energy points. Someone who understands energy centers can use these points to treat an animal who's in shock.

Each animal chakra does correspond to a position on the physical body. Unlike the chakras in people, however, animal chakras are not placed in a straight line down the body's center, as you'll see in the illustrations below.

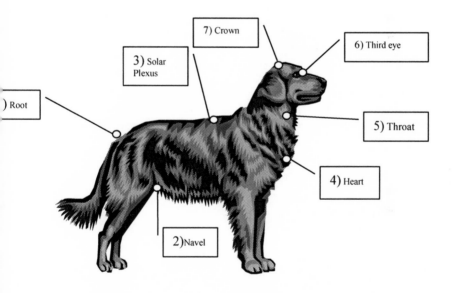

The chakra locations of several other animals with different body configurations are shown on the next page.

Visualizing chakra colors

When you're balancing the chakras for the purpose of healing, you'll use the specific color associated with each one at the appropriate time. Learning to do this is easy and requires only a little practice.

Sit quietly in a meditative state with your eyes lightly closed. In this state of heightened awareness, focus your attention on receiving the healing white light of the universe.

Next, you're going to visualize the white light changing from one color to another. Begin by seeing the light transformed to yellow. At first it may be a very pale yellow, but as you continue to observe it, you'll see it become more bold and intense. Once you clearly see the yellow light, change the color of that light energy to orange in your mind's eye. Again the orange will appear faint at first, but gradually it will become bold, solid and deep.

Continue transforming the universal white light energy into each of the chakra colors one at a time—yellow, orange, red, green, blue, indigo and violet—until you become comfortable with this visualization process. You'll soon realize that by simply changing your intention you can change the color. Once you've learned to do that, you'll be ready to help balance your pet's chakras by sending him the healing light of the universe using the appropriate color.

The following list may help you identify which chakra needs the most work and what associated color to use. You'll find an even more detailed list of information about each chakra toward the end of this chapter.

Color	Chakra	Associated With
Red	1st (root)	Reproductive organs, urinary tract, rectal area, red blood cells
Orange	2nd (navel area)	Kidneys, spleen, colon
Yellow	3rd (solar plexus)	Digestive system, liver, stomach, lymph system
Green	4th (heart area)	Heart, lungs, thymus
Blue	5th (throat area)	Thyroid, larynx, jaws, tonsils, mouth, speech
Indigo	6th (third eye area)	Eyes, brow, headaches, hormonal imbalance, developmental disorders
Violet	7th (crown)	Headaches, depression, mental deficiencies, imbalances, nerves, cancer

Your intention to heal, together with the visualization and transmission of color, will work wonders if you complete the healing process by also visualizing your pet receiving the light energy in the right places within his or her body, and putting it to good use.

Using the chakras in healing

You can use Cosmic Healing, in combination with the chakras, simply by sending the Universal Light energy to each chakra location as shown in the diagrams above.

Before you begin your energy work, you and your pet need to find a quiet place. First, gently massage each energy center, from the Root Chakra to the Crown Chakra, to allow the animal to relax and be able to tune in to the vibration of the energy you're going to be sending. You can massage in the appropriate direction by remembering that each energy center, or chakra, functions like a vortex that spins clockwise for males and counter-clockwise for females, as you're looking directly at them.

When your pet is relaxed, hold your hands in the "why?" position and wait for the healing energy to manifest within you through the prickling sensation you feel in the palms of your hands. *(The method for using Cosmic Healing was described in detail in the chapter about Energetic Healing, and exercises for learning to feel energy were described in the chapter about Auras if you need to review them.)*

Once you're comfortable and know that this is taking place, turn the palms of your hands towards your animal and begin letting the energy flow into each of their primary chakras, while imagining each chakra vortex spinning -- clockwise for males and counter-clockwise for females.

Always begin at the first, or Root, chakra at the base of the tail. Then proceed to each of the other chakras, in order, as you open and balance each area. *(In Cosmic Healing, remember that your hands are not usually touching your pet directly, although they may be if you feel intuitively guided to do so.)*

Since a specific color is associated with each chakra, send the color corresponding to each one by picturing the healing light changing shades as you move your hands from chakra point to chakra point on the animal's body.

You can send a particular color to your pet as if you're sending a burst of light energy. When you clearly see the color you want to use, think of this light energy as a colored ball. Visualize the area of the body you want to balance along with its associated chakra. Then with a burst of intent, send the colored light all at once to your pet, as if you were throwing the ball at him to play.

As you do this, you're sending a powerful thought that is energized with the appropriate color. See how the light enters your pet's body and how the cells begin utilizing that healing light. As you continue visualizing each color, the vortex of that chakra will increase in vitality and the color will intensify, even if you can't see this happening.

Remember: Always treat all seven chakras during every treatment because your goal is to achieve overall balance. It may take just a little bit longer to treat an individual chakra that needs more attention than the rest of them do, but each chakra needs to be well balanced before you end each treatment.

Once you've sent healing energy to each individual chakra, then visualize the healing light once again as almost a transparent and shimmering milky white light that now covers your pet's entire body. When you've completely finished treating your pet, remember to place the palms of your hands on your own face and breathe in deeply to receive any remaining light and healing energy for yourself. Know that you're an active participant in the healing of your pet, and release by giving thanks to the Universe for this powerful tool of loving, healing light.

Twenty minutes is a good length of time to allocate for a healing treatment. Often animals become sleepy during and after a treatment, but most of them will become energized and hungry when they're done. You might be, too!

Chakra associations

The following list will provide you with many interesting associations for each of the seven primary chakras.

Earlier in the chapter, I mentioned that an animal's thoughts and feelings filter down through the chakras to the animal's physical body where they manifest as certain behaviors or conditions. The explanations in the list below will identify some of these under the headings of *Unbalanced* and *Governs*. In addition to treating the appropriate chakra with healing light energy, you can then use the suggestions under the heading *To Awaken and Balance* to further help correct these imbalances.

Base/Root Chakra (1)

- Location: Base of spine
- Color: Red
- Gems: Ruby, red jasper, garnet, phantom red quartz crystal
- Note: C
- Glands: Adrenals
- Fragrance: Patchouli
- Element: Earth
- Planets: Saturn & Uranus
- Astrological Signs: Capricorn & Aquarius
- Symbol: Square
- Governs: Earthly grounding, physical survival, health, circulatory system
- Unbalanced: Anger, depression, survival fears, constipation, weight problems
- To Awaken and Balance: Animals, especially cats, should spend some time each day sitting directly in contact with the earth. Walk, run, hike, ride and even dance with them!

Navel/Spleen Chakra (2)

- Location: Reproductive system, womb, genitals
- Color: Orange
- Gems: Amber, carnelian, moonstone, topaz, fire opal
- Note: D
- Glands: Ovaries & testicles
- Fragrance: Musk
- Element: Water
- Planets: Jupiter & Neptune
- Astrological Signs: Sagittarius & Pisces

- Symbol: Pyramid
- Governs: Creativity, sexual energy, pleasure, desire and emotions, reproductive system
- Unbalanced: Jealousy, sexual problems, possessiveness, back pain, uterine or bladder problems
- To Awaken and Balance: Find an activity for your pet that requires lots of energy.

Solar Plexus Chakra (3)

- Location: On humans, between the navel and the lower part of the ribcage; On animals, on top of the back, in about the middle of the spine
- Color: Yellow
- Note: E
- Gems: Gold, tiger's eye, citrine, amber
- Glands: Pancreas & adrenals
- Fragrance: Rosemary
- Element: Fire
- Planets: Mars & Pluto
- Astrological Signs: Scorpio & Aries
- Symbol: Circle
- Governs: Emotions, perceptions, instincts, digestive system; considered the center of empathy; attunes people and animals to nature.
- Unbalanced: Stomach ailments, ulcers, diabetes, hypoglycemia, poor digestion, eating disorders, lack of will, anger, aggression, overemphasis on control
- To Awaken and Balance: Rub the top of the animal's spine, as well as his or her belly *(Because a chakra permeates the body, and because some animals show their tummies as an expression of submission, it's important to touch both sides of the animal's body.)*; become aware of the energy radiating from it's solar plexus; sit next to the pet and breathe using *your* diaphragm.

Note: This is one of the most important chakras for animals. Pictures of past events and first impressions are stored here.

Heart Chakra (4)

- Location: Center of the chest
- Color: Green.
- Note: F
- Gems: Green jade, emerald, malachite, rose quartz
- Gland: Thymus
- Fragrances: Amber and/or Sandalwood.
- Element: Air
- Planet: Venus
- Astrological Signs: Libra & Taurus
- Symbol: Cross
- Governs: Unconditional love, forgiveness, tolerance, compassion, immune system
- Unbalanced: Self hate, self mutilation, jealousy, lack of love, heart problems, asthma, high blood pressure, lung disease
- To Awaken and Balance: Give your pet opportunities to be of service to others by letting them bring enjoyment to other people and even to other pets.

Throat Chakra (5)

- Location: Near the thyroid gland on the throat
- Color: Blue
- Note: G
- Gems: Blue topaz, lapis lazuli, blue quartz, sodalite, turquoise
- Gland: Thyroid
- Attributes: Communication, expression, eloquence
- Fragrances: Clary Sage
- Element: Akasha and/or Ether
- Planet: Mercury
- Astrological Signs: Virgo & Gemini
- Symbol: Chalice (cup)
- Governs: Communications (barking, meowing, etc.), psychic hearing, expression, respiratory system
- Unbalanced: Tunnel vision, fixations, sore throat, stiff neck, thyroid and hearing problems

- To Awaken and Balance: Sing, chant, hum, and breathe consciously to soothe your pet and promote healing.

Note: In animals, this is the least developed chakra since they communicate telepathically.

Third Eye/Brow Chakra (6)

- Location: Between the eyes but a little higher
- Color: Indigo/violet
- Note: A
- Gems: Amethyst, turquoise, star/blue sapphire, tourmaline, clear quartz crystal
- Gland: Pineal
- Fragrance: Vanilla
- Element: Telepathic energy
- Planets: Sun & Moon
- Astrological signs: Cancer & Leo
- Symbol: Star of David
- Governs: Concentration, wisdom, mental faculties, pituitary and endocrine system
- Unbalanced: Lack of clarity, poor eyesight, headaches, lack of concentration
- To Awaken and Balance: Since this is a center of intuition, practice sending and receiving information from your pet.

Crown Chakra (7)

- Location: Top of the head at a point between the ears
- Color: Violet
- Note: B
- Gems: Amethyst, diamond, quartz crystal
- Gland: Pituitary
- Fragrance: Lotus
- Element: Cosmic Energy
- Planet: The Universe/Cosmos Astrological Signs: Higher expression of *all* signs
- Symbol: Lotus

- Governs: Nervous system; connection to our higher selves and the divine
- Unbalanced: Depression, lack of will, lack of spiritual attunement, apathy
- To Awaken and Balance: Meditate with your pet using guided visualizations to see health returning.

Note: In animals, the third eye and the crown chakras are combined because animals operate at psychic levels and are totally connected with God, the earth and the Universe.

Some closing thoughts

In the first four chapters of this book, you've learned about the importance of paying close attention to your intuition, the role of meditation, and some how-to techniques for communicating with your pets about everyday things and about health issues.

The next two chapters introduced you to spiritual ways in which you can help your pets heal by using prayer, affirmations, visualization, intention, Reiki, Cosmic Healing, and remote healing.

Now, after reading the chapters about auras and chakras, you've learned how energy, in the form of thoughts and feelings, flows through the four auras of your spiritual essence, and is then transferred through the chakras, so that it can be manifested in your body (your visible physical form), and that the same is true for your pets.

You've also learned techniques for bringing about healing in these energy layers that you can use both for your pets and for yourself.

Hopefully, the first eight chapters of the book have provided you with a solid foundation for helping your pets heal on a spiritual level. We'll look next at some guided meditations that may also be helpful for healing your pets spiritually.

Chapter 9

Guided Meditations For Healing

Introduction

A guided meditation is one that provides a script of calming and practical visualizations you can follow anytime you choose. This type of meditation is useful for someone who's just learning to meditate, or for anyone who'd like to discover some fresh new ideas.

It's important to remember, though, that the script of a guided meditation is meant to be only a guide. It's not something absolute that has to be followed in every detail. Always be sure to let your intuition show you what's best, and always follow your inner guidance, regardless of what the script says.

Each of the six guided meditations do share much of the same wording at the beginning and the end, but I've written everything out in full for each one so that whichever script you choose, it's complete in itself.

Several of these guided meditations have already been recorded on a prepared CD or audiocassette (available through www.petcommunicator.com). However, you might like to create your own tape or CD by reading them aloud yourself. For simplicity, I've alternated between the use of "him" or "her" whenever I'm referring to a pet, so you may need to change the pronoun to match the gender of your own pet as you're recording. After you've used the scripts for a while, you'll then be able to do these meditations entirely by yourself without the help of any tape or CD.

The purpose of each meditation

You'll use Guided Meditation 1 when you want to examine your pet's body to find out what may be wrong, or where your pet is hurting.

In Guided Meditation 2, you'll find detailed visualizations to help you send healing energy to your pet who's suffering from an illness, or who's recovering from surgery.

Guided Meditation 3 will lead you through the healing of present issues.

Meditation 4 will help you heal problems that have their roots in your pet's past.

Meditation 5 will enable you to prepare your pets for future events.

Guided Meditation 6 will help you talk with your pets who have already made their transitions into Spirit.

General meditation guidelines

You'll begin as you would for any meditation, by focusing on your breathing, and quieting your mind so that you can let the healing energy of Spirit's love flow through you. As the script unfolds naturally, you're then able to relax more deeply and focus on the thoughts being presented.

Once your mind is quiet, you'll find yourself in a tranquil garden filled with bushes, plants and flowers of every variety. This is the place of **The Present Moment**. It's where you'll begin and end your meditation each time. As beautiful as your garden is, though, you're eager to follow the path you see at the far side.

Every time you arrive at the end of this tree and flower-lined path, you'll come into a special place of your choice where you can spiritually meet and commune with your pet.

This may be a place of natural beauty like a park, an out of the way mountain top, a far away island with a majestic waterfall, near a river where you enjoy watching the rapids, at a secluded beach, or any other place of beauty and serenity. It may also be a make-believe place which no one else has ever seen, like a space healing station located somewhere in the universe.

Whatever place you choose, it's always one where you feel very safe and secure, and just being there calms your spirit, or sends it soaring with joy. This is the place we'll call **The Now**.

Next, you'll mentally ask your pet to come to you in a spiritual way. During your conversation, ask him all of the questions you want.

When you're asking him questions, listen openly with all of your senses. Accept the information exactly as it's presented to you. Don't try to make it become something *you* think it should be. You're simply like a radio or a TV that receives a signal *exactly* as it's being sent.

Sometimes you'll need to wait silently for a little while until an answer comes. Other times, the information you receive may come very fast, and it may be difficult to focus on it for as long as you'd like, but keep going, knowing that you *will* recall all that you need to remember.

Occasionally you may even feel as if you haven't received any clear answer at all. When this happens, try asking the question again. If the answer still doesn't become clear to you after a few more tries, move on to another topic. You may be trying *too* hard to listen for the answer *you* think you should hear. Doing so may keep you from hearing what your pet is actually trying to tell you. You can always come back and try asking the same question at a later time. Once in a while, though, your pet may not want to give you a specific answer, and it's important to respect that.

If you need to tell your pet something, especially about an event that will be happening in the future, send him pictures that are as clear and detailed as you can possibly make them.

You'll be sending the healing energy of the Universe to your pet during your meditation, so plan to spend all the time you need in your special place.

When you're both finished, you'll send him on his way, enjoy a few more quiet moments in your chosen place, and then walk back along the path into the garden of **The Present Moment**.

You'll pause in this tranquil garden again, but only briefly because it's now time to end your meditation. You'll notice that you're beginning to breathe more deeply, and you're becoming consciously aware of your body as you wiggle your toes and stretch your arms and legs. Your eyes open and you're once again fully and completely aware of the current surroundings of your everyday life.

Having a tape recorder turned on while you meditate may be helpful so that you can record as many of your observations as possible. This way, you'll still be able to keep your eyes closed and more easily remain in your meditative state than you could if you were trying to take written notes.

A special note about Meditations 3, 4, 5 and 6

Since meditations 3, 4, 5 and 6 (present, past, future, and in Spirit) are somewhat similar, let's take a moment to see what's specific to each type.

It's in The Now where you'll first ask your pet to meet you, and spend time communing with you spiritually in each of the meditations.

It's also in The Now that you'll work on resolving physical, emotional or spiritual challenges, or help your pet make behavioral changes, if the problems started in the present time.

But, while you're in **The Now**, you'll also notice that there's a bridge to your *left*, another bridge to your *right*, and a third bridge in the *center*, off in the distance.

The bridge to the left represents The Past. This is the bridge the two of you will take together from **The Now** whenever you want to resolve a current behavior problem that may have had its origin somewhere in your pet's past. On the other side of this bridge, you'll find yourself in a completely different part of your favorite place, or you may even decide to select an entirely new location altogether—one which is also very beautiful and special to you. But no matter which place of peace and serenity you choose, every time you cross the bridge to your *left*, you'll both have a sense that you're taking a walk *back* in time.

The bridge to the right represents The Future. This is the bridge the two of you will take together from **The Now** whenever you need to talk about something that's *going* to be happening. On the other side of this bridge, you'll find yourself in yet another completely different part of your favorite place, or, to talk about future events you may even want to go to an entirely new location that has special significance for you. But no matter which place of peace and serenity you choose, every time you cross the bridge to your *right*, you'll both have a sense that you're taking a walk *forward* in time.

The center bridge in the distance is the Rainbow Bridge into Spirit, and it's the one you'll use to go talk with your pets who have already made their transitions. You'll be able to talk with any pets who are now in Spirit, no matter how long ago they left their physical bodies.

Working in two different time frames during the same meditation

There may be times when you've started talking with your pet in **The Now,** but it suddenly dawns on you that the cause of the problem may not have it's origin in the present at all. Possibly the reason for the current inappropriate behavior stems from an unpleasant experience that took place some time ago.

This could be something from earlier in your pet's life if you raised him from puppyhood. Or, if you adopted an older pet, you may definitely need to look further into his or her past to find the root cause of the current behavior problem.

If this should happen, in your mind's eye, simply ask your pet to walk with you over the bridge to your left. You can then walk slowly together, or sit quietly in the silence in this place of beauty and try to discover the real reason why your pet seems to be having difficulty at the present time.

Or, in another scenario, you may already be working in **The Now,** and realize you need to tell your pet that the very same activity the two of you are talking about at the moment will also be happening again in the future. In this case, ask your pet to walk with you over the bridge to your *right.* When he understands that you want to talk to him about something that's *going* to be happening, send him clear and vivid pictures showing him all the details.

It's important to understand that each of your pet's issues (physical, emotional, spiritual or behavioral) has its *origin* in a specific time frame, whether it's something that's happening now, something that happened in your pet's past, or something that will be happening in the future. By working together in the time frame that applies, you'll be better able to address the *original cause* of the problem. When you do this, a more complete healing can take place.

While you might be able to communicate successfully the ideas of past or future to your pet, even from **The Now,** you may find that mentally crossing over one of the bridges, for at least a few moments, helps both of you to better focus on the specific time frame.

The main thing to keep in mind is that you'll want to do whatever comes naturally to you when you're doing this type of meditation. That may mean remaining in one place and sending your pet clear thoughts to show which time frame you're talking about, or it might mean that you'll want to get up and walk across the appropriate bridge in your mind's eye.

Some closing thoughts

Now that you've had an overview of each type of guided meditation, you're ready to choose the one that will be most appropriate for you.

Your pet doesn't actually have to be present with you when you're talking together spiritually, though often he or she may enjoy lying nearby while you meditate.

Remember that whenever you're meditating, your mind should become like the waters of a very calm and placid lake. To achieve that kind of stillness, you must always set your own conscious thoughts aside first. Then you'll be able to clearly receive all of the thoughts your pet wants to send you.

As you use each of these guided meditations, you'll soon discover that they'll bring you closer to your pet than you ever expected, as well as giving *you* a sense of accomplishment and peace of mind.

Chapter 10

Guided Meditation I

Discovering What's Wrong with Your Pet Or Where It Hurts

In this meditation you're going to ask your pet to let you examine her body, inside and out, from head to toe, to try to discover the cause of her discomfort or pain.

How will you know if there's a problem in some part of her body? Possibly you'll see a colored light in that area. The color and size of the light you see may be an indication of the seriousness of the problem. The light might be yellow if something is just developing, or red if it's already more advanced. It may be small, like a pinpoint, or larger and glowing. It may even be pulsating.

If you don't have time to do a thorough organ by organ scan, simply ask your pet for permission to look inside her body, as if you're looking at an x-ray of her insides from head to tail. While you're scanning the "x-ray," again look for lights of various colors and intensities to help you know where the problem or problems might be.

Meditation: Discovering What's Wrong

Find a comfortable and very quiet place to sit, a spot where you won't be disturbed by people talking, telephones ringing, TV or music playing, or other interruptions.

Remove your shoes, and loosen any clothing that feels too tight.

If you're sitting on the ground in an attitude of contemplation, be sure to keep your back straight. If this is difficult for you to do, sit against a wall for support.

If you're sitting on a chair or on a sofa, let your back be supported by the furniture. Your feet should be resting, uncrossed, flat on the ground.

105

Place your hands on your lap, palms up, with the fingers of one hand resting on top of the fingers of the other hand, and the tips of your thumbs gently touching, forming a circle.

Close your eyes and become conscious of your breathing. Breathe deeply at first with your mouth closed, inhaling only through your nose. Then with your mouth slightly open, exhale slowly. Hear the soft whoosh of air as you're exhaling it out. Do this seven times.

With each inhaled breath of pure, refreshing air, feel yourself becoming calmer. As you exhale, release any random thoughts and any tension you've acquired during the day. Let your body become more and more deeply relaxed with every breath, in and out.

As your breathing now becomes deeper and slower, consciously begin to relax each part of your body.

Become aware of your face as the tension drifts away and your facial muscles become more relaxed . . . in your forehead . . . eyebrows . . . eyelids . . . eyes . . . cheeks . . . jaw . . . and lips.

Your facial muscles are now so relaxed that you may even feel yourself smiling.

Let your tongue roll upward and rest gently on the roof of your mouth, forming a circle inside of your body to correspond to the circle you formed with your hands on the outside of your body.

Become aware of the tension releasing from your neck . . . shoulders . . . arms . . . and hands. You should feel your shoulders drop slightly as the tension drifts away. Feel the sense of calming relaxation flow all the way down your arms, through your hands, and out to your fingertips.

Let your breathing naturally become more shallow and rhythmic.

Become aware of the relaxation flowing gently through the main part of your body . . . through the areas of your chest and upper back . . . your abdomen and lower back . . . through your hips and buttocks . . . and thighs.

Let it continue flowing down through your lower legs . . . through your feet . . . and all the way to the tips of your toes.

Continue to breathe at a naturally slower and more relaxed pace as you experience a wonderful sense of total relaxation.

If your mind wanders, calmly bring yourself back by focusing your attention on the gentle rhythm of your breathing.

Next, before you go further, take a complete inventory of any pain or discomfort you're aware of anywhere in your own body.

> (It's very important to know what feelings of discomfort belong to you, before you begin to check your pet's body, so check yourself externally and internally from head to toe first.)

Once you know what feelings belong to you, then visualize that you're extending strong roots from the soles of your feet deep down into Mother Earth. Just as a wise old tree does, these roots burrow deep into the ground beneath your feet and spread out to find nourishment and water, the symbol of life energy.

With your third eye (your spiritual eye, located between your eyebrows), *look upward. See a wonderful, shimmering white light coming down from the heavens straight to you. It's the light of the Universe. It's the all-knowing, all-seeing light, and it's here for you, for your benefit and the benefit of your pets. In it is all the wisdom you need to have available to you at this moment.*

Feel the warmth of this loving energy as it gently enters through the top of your head and fills your entire being all the way to the tips of your toes. So much loving light flows through you that what you cannot hold overflows from the top of your head like a fountain. Your entire body, inside and out, is now bathed in this loving light.

This stream of light energy will continue to flow through and around you during your entire meditation to envelop you, both inside and out, in it's loving, healing care. You're very relaxed, and feeling very nurtured.

Breathe gently as you take a few moments to let yourself totally experience all the loving tenderness of the healing light of the Universe.

Now envision yourself in a tranquil garden setting. Flowers, plants and bushes of every variety create a feast for the eyes and spirit. Colors of every shade and hue, both soft and vibrant, fill you with a sense of peace and joy. Fragrances waft on the gentle breeze, while the sun sparkles through the trees. This is **The Present Moment**. *Allow yourself some precious time to let its beauty permeate all of your senses.*

As beautiful as everything is, though, you're eager to follow the tree-lined path you see at the far side of the garden. It, too, is abundant with natural beauty.

Notice the firm support of the earth under your feet as you're walking.

Feel the gentle breeze as it touches your face and arms.

Observe the vibrant colors of all the bushes and flowers you see along the way. Smell their delightful fragrances. Notice the shapes and sizes of any rocks and stones, and feel the smoothness or roughness of their textures. Hear the clean, clear, fresh water running in a nearby brook or stream.

Feel yourself being the joyful, balanced, well grounded person you truly are at the very center of your being.

Allow yourself to experience your gifts of inner beauty, inner strength, and inner wisdom.

Know that in your spirit you're a beautiful reflection of the One who created you.

As you approach the end of this path, you discover that it's led you right into one of your favorite places where you like to spend time. This may be a place in nature like a park, an out of the way mountain top, a far away island with a majestic waterfall, near a river where you enjoy watching the rapids, at a secluded beach, or any other place of beauty and serenity. It may also be a make-believe place which no one else has ever seen, like a space healing station located somewhere in the universe.

Whatever place you choose, it's always one where you feel very safe and secure, and just being there calms your spirit, or sends it soaring with joy. This is the place we call **The Now.**

Find a comfortable place to sit and allow yourself time to absorb every detail in all of the beauty that surrounds you. Notice the light . . . the colors . . . the fragrances . . . the sounds . . . the sizes . . . the shapes . . . the textures. Look . . . listen . . . touch . . . enjoy. Let yourself become intimately familiar with everything about your special place.

As you bask in this beautiful paradise, remember that this is your safe place. You may come here anytime you need to relax. No one else is allowed here unless you offer a special invitation.

When you're ready, picture your pet in your mind and call her by name. Ask her to come and spend some spiritual time with you.

Observe your pet carefully as she comes closer to you. In your mind's eye, notice every detail.

What's the expression in her eyes? Are they clear and bright?

Look at her ears. Do they move when she walks?

Is her tail wagging, and is she happy to see you?

When she's approaching you, is she walking calmly, or is she running quickly toward you?

Make sure you're observing everything. Remember, your eyes are closed and you're experiencing all of these images only in your mind and heart. This is also true for anything you mentally touch.

Feel her fur and note its condition. Is it soft and silky, wiry or curly, lustrous and shiny?

Look into her eyes. Tell her how much you love her. Can you see the love in her eyes for you?

Greet her as you normally would, telling her how much you love her. Send your love to her as a ray of light from your heart to hers.

Tell her that you would very much like to find out how to help her feel better, and ask her permission to let you examine her body, both inside and out.

At this point, "become" your pet for a moment by virtually letting your spirit enter into her body so that you can better experience whatever she's feeling, both externally and internally.

Imagine your spirit temporarily leaving your body through the top of your head. Since your spirit isn't constrained by any particular physical size or shape, see it becoming very, very small so that you can easily "be" inside the body of your pet. Enter her body through the top of her head, maybe even wiggling yourself in as if you were trying on a very snug sweater.

Once you're comfortably "inside," quietly observe everything, ask questions, and wait for her replies, knowing that you'll be able to remember everything she says.

Check the outer part of her body first and note any new feelings you experience in the corresponding part of your own body.

Does she have any headaches, shoulder aches, upper or lower backaches? Is her spine naturally aligned? Is her back flexible? Can her tail move freely and easily?

Observe her extremities. Experience, in the soles of your own feet, anything she might be feeling on, or between, the pads of her paws, or around her toenails.

Check her upper and lower legs and knees. Does she have any pain, sore spots, malformations, lumps, bumps or any other kind of discomfort?

When she bends each leg, does she do so easily, or only with difficulty? Does it hurt? Does it make a noise, as if the bones are rubbing against each other?

Feel yourself, as your pet, walking on all four paws. Is her gait smooth? Does she hurt anywhere? Does she tend to lean more to one side or the other? Does she favor any particular leg? Do her hips move freely and easily?

Is she able to lie down naturally, and able to stand up again easily after lying down for some length of time?

Check all of her outer body and extremities for stiffness, muscle problems, circulation, or foreign masses.

Move to the inside of her body now and explore each of her internal organs. Check her brain . . . her hearing . . . her vision . . . her ability to smell and taste. Observe her heart . . . lungs . . . stomach . . . liver . . . and kidneys.

As you observe each of the organs, note how you feel in your own body. Is her heart racing or skipping a beat? Does she feel like gasping for air? Does she have any burning sensation when she urinates? Are there any obstructions anywhere? Does she have too much acid in her stomach or have difficulty digesting food? Is there anything making her sick, itchy, or uncomfortable?

Remember that all of your senses are working together. You may feel things in your own body, see the shape of something growing, hear a "yes" or a "no" coming from your pet, smell a food that makes her sick, or smell the odor of an infection, or you may touch something like grass under her paws and know how that makes her feel, and you may taste food that she loves, or that doesn't agree with her. Sensory perception will give you a lot of information. Accept everything without doubting it.

When you're satisfied that your examination is complete and that all of your questions have been answered, gently let your spirit lift out through the top of her head and re-enter your own body through the top of your head.

*Take a moment to realize, with assurance, that any aches or pains you felt during this time belonged to your pet, and **not** to your own body. **Release all of those feelings**, so that once again the only feelings you experience are your own.*

Thank your pet for spending this special time with you, and tell her how much you love her and want to help her. Let her know that the two of you can do this again whenever she has something she needs to show you. Then send her on her way in your mind's eye. You may see her walk away, or she may simply disappear.

Having accomplished what you set out to do, spend a few additional quiet, peaceful moments in your special place by yourself. Know that you can return any time you wish, and that the joy and beauty you've experienced will always be here for you.

It's then time to say farewell to your special place of peace and serenity in **The Now** *and prepare to return to* **The Present Moment** *in the tranquil garden, so begin walking back along the path that originally brought you here.*

Continue to experience all of the vibrant colors, fragrant scents, and beautiful sights. Notice again the textures, shapes and sizes of the rocks and stones you observed when you first walked this path . . . hear the sound of the water in the brook or stream fading more and more softly into the distance.

Follow the path until you arrive back in the peaceful garden where you began this journey. Enjoy the beauty once again, but only for a few moments this time, because you're now ready to return to your normal state of awareness.

Feel yourself in your sitting position. Let the roots you put down into Mother Earth recede back into the soles of your feet. Visualize how they're absorbed perfectly back inside of your body as they become smaller and smaller. Wiggle your toes and become even more consciously aware of your body.

Give thanks for the beautiful healing energy that surrounds and permeates every part of your being. Then let it travel upward and exit through the top of your head. See how it blends into the heavens and know that it will always be there for you anytime you need it.

Now become completely aware of your physical body and the present time. Stretch luxuriously, feeling rested and joyful.

Breathe deeply and give thanks.

If necessary, count from one to five, becoming much more alert, aware, and physically active with each successive number . . . and when you're ready, open your eyes.

Chapter 11

Guided Meditation 2

Helping to Heal Illness
Or to Speed Recovery Following Surgery

This healing meditation is helpful for a pet who's been through major surgery of any kind, or for one who has a condition or a disease which veterinary medicine doesn't seem to be able to help. It grew out of an experience I had with one of my own dogs.

Chop Chop, my precious Shih-Tzu, suffered severely from hip dysplasia when he was barely two years old. He'd stopped walking altogether and his gaze was fixed on the horizon. He no longer wanted to be petted, and didn't seem to recognize me when I talked to him. Consultations with two different veterinarians indicated that the prognosis was grim.

One night, I lay next to him on the floor feeling drained from crying, and flooded with grief because I feared that I was going to lose him soon. As we lay quietly side by side, I clearly heard him say to me, "You call yourself a healer . . . you've helped a lot of humans . . . so do something!"

For quite some time, I'd been using a technique known as Cosmic Healing to bring healing energy to people, but until I heard Chop Chop's words, it hadn't ever occurred to me that I could use the same loving energy to help animals heal, too.

I immediately began sending him the healing energy of the Universe that evening, and several times the next day. The results were nothing short of miraculous. In the morning, following the evening treatment, he was standing on all fours and shaking his mane. This was something he hadn't been able to do for several days. Within a week, he returned to being his playful, active self -- for another twelve years! He was a happy and mobile senior citizen before finally crossing over the Rainbow Bridge at the age of 14.

The message I received from Chop Chop that day was a life changing moment, both for him and for me. He'd succeeded in showing me that not only should I be communicating with animals about everyday things and behavior problems, as I'd already been doing, but that it was now time for me to also be bringing them the loving energy of the Universe to help heal their physical, emotional and spiritual challenges as well.

Once Chop Chop recovered, it became clear to me that we don't need to feel hopeless and helpless when our pets are facing serious illness or injury, or trying to recover from major surgery. There **is** something we can do for them. If their appointed time hasn't yet come, they may respond very well to receiving healing energy. To do so, however, they still need to have the will to live, and they still need to have a purpose to fulfill in this life.

After my experience with Chop Chop, I developed the following healing meditation and have used it with great success to help quite a number of pets. You may also want to use it so that you, too, can *Do Something!*

At one point in this meditation, in your mind's eye, you'll be asking your pet to sit or lie down in front of you, but it would be a wonderful experience for both of you if your pet could also be physically present with you at the same time. This way, you could actually place your hands directly on your pet's body while you're visualizing placing your hands on your pet in your meditation.

Meditation: Healing illness
or speeding surgical recovery

Find a comfortable and very quiet place to sit, a spot where you won't be disturbed by people talking, telephones ringing, TV or music playing, or other interruptions.

Remove your shoes, and loosen any clothing that feels too tight.

If you're sitting on the ground in an attitude of contemplation, be sure to keep your back straight. If this is difficult for you to do, sit against a wall for support.

If you're sitting on a chair or on a sofa, let your back be supported by the furniture. Your feet should be resting, uncrossed, flat on the ground.

Place your hands on your lap, palms up, with the fingers of one hand resting on top of the fingers of the other hand, and the tips of your thumbs gently touching, forming a circle.

Close your eyes and become conscious of your breathing. Breathe deeply at first with your mouth closed, inhaling only through your nose. Then with your mouth slightly open, exhale slowly. Hear the soft whoosh of air as you're exhaling it out. Do this seven times.

With each inhaled breath of pure, refreshing air, feel yourself becoming calmer. As you exhale, release any random thoughts and any tension you've acquired during the day. Let your body become more and more deeply relaxed with every breath, in and out.

To deepen your relaxation, begin at the top of your head. Become aware of each part of your face, as the tension drifts away and your facial muscles become more relaxed . . . in your forehead . . . eyebrow area . . . eyelids . . . eyes . . . cheeks . . . jaw . . . and lips.

Your facial muscles are now so relaxed that you may even feel yourself smiling.

Let your tongue roll upward and gently rest on the roof of your mouth, forming a circle inside your body to correspond to the circle you formed with your hands on the outside of your body.

Become aware of the tension being released from your neck . . . shoulders . . . arms . . . and hands. You should feel your shoulders drop slightly as the tension drifts away. Feel the sense of calming relaxation flow all the way down your arms, through your hands, and out to your fingertips.

Let your breathing naturally become more shallow and rhythmic.

Become aware of the relaxation flowing gently through the main part of your body . . . through the areas of your chest and upper back . . . your abdomen and lower back . . . through your hips and buttocks . . . and thighs.

Let it continue flowing down through your lower legs . . . through your feet . . . and all the way to the tips of your toes.

Continue to breathe at a naturally slower and more relaxed pace as you experience a wonderful sense of total relaxation.

If your mind wanders, calmly bring yourself back by focusing your attention on the gentle rhythm of your breathing.

Now, visualize that, from the soles of your feet, you're growing strong roots deep down into Mother Earth. Just as a wise old tree does, these roots burrow deep into the ground beneath your feet and spread out to find nourishment and water, the symbol of life energy.

With your third eye (your spiritual eye, located between your eyebrows), *look upward. See a wonderful, shimmering white light coming down from the heavens straight to you. It's the light of the Universe. It's the all-knowing, all-seeing light and it's here for you, for your benefit and the benefit of your pets. In it is all the wisdom you need to have available to you at this moment.*

Feel the warmth of this loving energy as it gently enters through the top of your head and fills your entire being all the way to the tips of your toes. So much loving light flows through you that what you cannot hold overflows from the top of your head like a fountain. Your entire body, inside and out, is now bathed in this loving light.

This stream of light energy will continue to flow through and around you during your entire meditation to envelop you, both inside and out, in it's loving, healing care. You're very relaxed, and feeling very nurtured.

Breathe gently as you take a few moments to let yourself totally experience all the loving tenderness of the healing light of the Universe.

Now envision yourself in a tranquil garden setting. Flowers, plants and bushes of every variety create a feast for the eyes and spirit. Colors of every shade and hue, both soft and vibrant, fill you with a sense of peace and joy. Fragrances waft on the gentle breeze, while the sun sparkles through the trees. This is **The Present Moment**. *Allow yourself some precious time to let its beauty permeate all of your senses.*

As beautiful as everything is, though, you're eager to follow the tree-lined path you see at the far side of the garden. It, too, is abundant with natural beauty.

Notice the firm support of the earth under your feet as you're walking.

Feel the gentle breeze as it touches your face and arms.

Observe the vibrant colors of all the bushes and flowers you see along the way. Smell their delightful fragrances. Notice the shapes and sizes of any rocks and stones, and feel the smoothness or roughness of their textures. Hear the clean, clear, fresh water running in a nearby brook or stream.

Feel yourself being the joyful, balanced, well grounded person you truly are at the very center of your being.

Allow yourself to experience your gifts of inner beauty, inner strength, and inner wisdom.

Know that in your spirit you're a beautiful reflection of the One who created you.

As you approach the end of this path, you discover that it's led you right into one of your favorite places where you like to spend time. This may be a place in nature like a park, an out of the way mountain top, a far away island with a majestic waterfall, near a river where you enjoy watching the rapids, at a secluded beach, or any other place of beauty and serenity. It may also be a make-believe place which no one else has ever seen, like a space healing station located somewhere in the universe.

Whatever place you choose, it's always one where you feel very safe and secure, and just being there calms your spirit, or sends it soaring with joy. This is the place we call **The Now.**

Find a comfortable place to sit, and then continue to enjoy the stunning beauty of this, your very special place. Allow yourself time to absorb every detail in all of the beauty that surrounds you. Notice the light . . . the colors . . . all the fragrances . . . the sounds . . . the sizes . . . the shapes . . . the textures. Look . . . listen . . . touch . . . enjoy. Let yourself become intimately familiar with everything about your special place. Take it all in!

As you bask in this beautiful paradise, remember that this is your safe place. You may come here anytime you need to relax. No one else is allowed here unless you offer a special invitation.

When you're ready, picture your pet in your mind and call him by name. Ask him to come and spend some spiritual time with you.

Observe your pet carefully as he comes closer to you. In your mind's eye, notice every detail.

What's the expression in his eyes? Are they clear and bright?

Look at his ears. Do they move when he walks?

Is his tail wagging, and is he happy to see you?

When he's approaching you, is he walking calmly, or is he running quickly toward you?

Make sure you're observing everything. Remember, your eyes are closed, and you're experiencing all of these images, and anything you mentally touch, in your mind and heart.

Feel his fur and note its condition. Is it soft and silky, wiry or curly, lustrous or shiny?

Look into his eyes. Tell him how much you love him. Can you see the love in his eyes for you?

Tell your pet that you would like to help him heal from his illness or disability, or that you want to help him recover more quickly from his recent surgery. Ask him to sit or lie down in front of you.

This is also the time to ask others to help with your pet's healing. It may be someone who's still living, or someone who's already in Spirit, whether you know them or not. Ask for them by name, or by title, and see how they come to you from all directions. Call on all of the healers, all of the doctors, all of the friends your animal has, and ask them to come and sit close to you, and to him, forming a giant circle. They're all coming to help your precious pet heal.

Each person, including you, will have his or her hands extended palms down toward your pet, and at your request they'll all start letting the healing light of the Universe flow from the palms of their hands directly to him. (You may also put your hands physically on your pet at this time if he's present with you.)

If you know where the disease is located, or where the surgical site is, ask everyone to concentrate on that area first. Silently spend several minutes doing this.

Now, ask everyone to let the healing light flow to every part of your pet's body. Observe that where before there was pain or disease, there's now only loving healing energy filling his body with wholeness, completeness, balance and harmony.

If your pet has had surgery, imagine yourself threading a needle made of light. You're using a very fine thread that is also made of light. It's so fine you can hardly see it, but because the light glows, you know it's there.

Use the healing light of this needle and thread to "suture" right over the physical sutures from your pet's operation. When you're finished, leave the healing thread in place.

If your pet has had surgery, or has a disease, an infection, a wound, or an infirmity of any kind, take a sponge made of light that has been soaked in a healing solution and apply it over the area. Know that this healing light-filled solution will go through the fur, into the skin, and deep into his body to cure whatever needs healing. Also treat his whole body with the sponge soaked in the healing solution, especially if you don't know the exact location that needs to be healed.

Then, in your visualization, ask your pet to take a few sips of healing water from the stream nearby. As it travels throughout the inside of his system, know that healing is taking place in his body from the inside out.

Everyone who is assisting you has been sending healing light to your pet the entire time, and the same healing light that has been bathing your body, inside and out, has also been flowing to your pet through the palms of your hands.

Next, visualize yourself placing a blanket of healing light over your pet. Because this blanket is made of light energy, it conforms itself perfectly to the size of your pet's body and to his every curve. When you place it on him, it immediately fits so well that it looks like another coat of fur. But this light blanket is very special because it provides him with continuous healing energy. It will remain with him for as long as he needs it, until he's completely healed once again.

Know that with your visualizations you're doing everything you can to help him fully recover.

Thank everyone who came to help with your pet's healing, and ask them to continue sending loving healing energy to your pet even after they leave. Each of them will then return to his or her own time and space.

Spend a few moments alone now with your pet friend. While you're together in this special moment, know that your pet has received and absorbed all of the healing light and love from the Universe, and that this loving energy will continue to do its healing work within him. Share the silence together.

Now, send your love to your pet as a beautiful ray of light from your heart to his heart. Give him a kiss, remind him that his healing is taking place right now, and let him go on his way. You may see him walk away, or he may simply disappear.

Spend a few additional quiet, peaceful moments in your special place by yourself. Know that you can return any time you wish, and that the joy and beauty of your chosen place will always be here for you.

It's then time to say farewell to your special place of peace and serenity in **The Now** *and prepare to return to* **The Present Moment** *in the tranquil garden, so begin walking back along the path that originally brought you here.*

Continue to experience all of the vibrant colors, fragrant scents, and beautiful sights. Notice again the textures, shapes and sizes of the rocks and stones you observed when you first walked this path . . . hear the sound of the water in the brook or stream fading more and more softly into the distance.

Follow the path until you arrive back in the peaceful garden where you began this journey. Enjoy the beauty once again, but only for a few moments this time, because you're now ready to return to your normal state of awareness.

Feel yourself in your sitting position. Let the roots you put down into Mother Earth recede back into the soles of your feet. Visualize how they're absorbed perfectly back inside of your body as they become smaller and smaller. Wiggle your toes and become even more consciously aware of your body.

Give thanks for the beautiful healing energy that surrounds and permeates every part of your being. Then let it travel upward and exit through the top of your head. See how it blends into the heavens and know that it will always be there for you anytime you need it.

Now become fully aware of your physical body and the present time. Stretch luxuriously, feeling rested and joyful.

Breathe deeply and give thanks.

If necessary, count from one to five, becoming much more alert, aware and physically active with each successive number . . . and when you're ready, open your eyes.

Chapter 12

Guided Meditation 3

Healing the Present

In this meditation, you'll go in spirit to a beautiful place of your choice which we'll call **The Now**. You can spend time in **The Now**, to treat a physical, emotional or spiritual problem, or to ask your pet to make a behavioral change.

Behavioral changes could have something to do with how your pet relates to a person or another animal. Or they might be about a behavior that needs to be changed, like leaving food alone when it's meant for people and not for pets, staying on the floor instead of getting up on a sofa, chair or bed, or using the outdoors to go potty instead of going in the house.

When you're working in **The Now**, you can also "train" your pet through the pictures you send. For example, if you've just put in a new doggy door, you can mentally show your pet how to use it to go out, and how to come back in again. If it won't be open all the time, you can explain why it will sometimes be closed.

You may also need to talk about why you're making a change in your pet's diet if she develops allergies or needs to lose weight.

Maybe you'll need to talk about a change of some kind in the usual daily routine, if for instance, your pet needs to fast before having a medical test, or if you start working different hours and, therefore, feeding or walking her at different times.

You'll also want to use this time to ask your pet if there's anything special he or she needs from you.

Working in two different time frames if necessary

In the Introduction you learned that there are several bridges in **The Now** that you can use at the appropriate times.

Sometimes, when you're already working in **The Now**, you may discover that what you and your pet are talking about actually has its roots in your pet's past or it needs to be explained as something that will be happening sometime in the near future.

If this happens, feel free to get up from your position in **The Now** and walk together with your pet across either the bridge to **The Past** or the bridge to **The Future**. Stay there as long as you need to, and when you're finished, come back across the bridge together into **The Now**.

A side trip to The Future

When you're already in **The Now**, you may discover that what you and your pet are talking about also needs to be addressed in **The Future**.

This would be particularly true if you're trying to heal a recurring issue like your pet acting scared or behaving defensively every time family and friends come to visit, or not eating when the pet sitter comes while you're on vacation.

To work on this type of problem, ask your pet to walk together with you over the bridge to your right into **The Future**.

This new location can be a completely different part of your favorite place, or you may even want to go to an entirely new location, one that has special significance for you. The important thing is that by crossing the bridge to **The Future**, you'll both have the sense that you're now taking a walk forward in time.

Spend a few moments exploring the beauty you find on the other side of the bridge, then walk slowly together or find a comfortable place to sit. Mentally, send your pet words and visual pictures, filled with every possible detail, which will help her understand whatever it is she needs to know about what's going to be happening, and how you want her to act in these circumstances.

Ask her if she understands. Ask her to tell you how she feels about changing her behavior. What can she do to be an active participant when the time comes? Is there anything you can do to help her more easily adjust to what she needs to do in the future?

When you're both finished, thank her for listening and understanding and, together, walk back over the bridge into **The Now**.

A side trip to The Past

If at any time you have the feeling that a physical, emotional or spiritual problem has it's origins in the near or distant past, ask your pet to walk with you over the bridge to your left.

This new location can also be another part of your favorite place, or it can be an entirely different scene of your choosing -- one which is also very beautiful and special to you. The important thing is that by crossing the bridge to **The Past**, you'll both have the sense that you're now taking a walk back in time.

While both of you are in **The Past**, observe the beauty of your new surroundings, then walk slowly together or sit quietly in the silence. Let your pet know you want to help her, but in order to do so, you need to better understand what happened to her in an earlier part of her life.

Ask her to tell you about things she previously experienced that might be causing her to have a problem now.

Let your mind relax as you wait for some kind of communication: a picture, a feeling, a smell or a taste sensation that she sends you. Pay special attention to anything you feel in your own body, or see or hear in your mind's eye. Your pet may tell you something that will help you understand her previous experiences. If the information you receive is something you wouldn't have thought of on your own, then it's no doubt definitely something your pet is telling you.

If your pet is willing and able to share specific information with you about events in her past history, then you'll be able to explain to her what she needs to know so that she can change her perception about the present.

Offer her some solutions, and wait for her to respond. Maybe all she needs is reassurance from you that the home she's living in now is her permanent home, and you'll always provide her with the love and care she needs.

If you're able to receive some help from her, thank her, and tell her you now have a much better understanding of her situation.

What if you don't seem to receive
any thoughts from your pet?

Sometimes, as a beginner, you may feel as if you aren't receiving any helpful information, especially when you're talking to your pet about her past. You may be expecting to clearly hear a voice, or see a detailed videotape of what happened, or receive definite ideas about what you should be doing to help her. But sometimes the feelings or pictures your pet sends are so subtle that you may think nothing's happening.

This isn't true. Please know that even if you feel *you* aren't receiving anything, your pet most likely *is* receiving pictures from you. Our thoughts and feelings are easy for pets to read, so just know that while the sharing of information might seem one sided at the moment, in time, and with practice, you too will be able to receive information.

When you seem to be having difficulty seeing, hearing or feeling anything, wait quietly as long as you can maintain your focus. That means not letting any other thoughts wander into your mind. When or if they do, it means that you haven't yet reached a deep enough level of meditation necessary to experience these new feelings, sensations and images. Simply let it go, and don't be concerned about it for now. Just know that with practice and patience it will happen.

Again, your pet will understand the concern you've shared with her and you'll soon see that there'll be a slight difference, not only in how your pet approaches the problem, but also in how you see it.

Thank your pet for listening to what you had to say and reassure her that you'll still do all you can to help her understand whatever it is she needs to know.

When you're both finished talking about her past, then walk back over the bridge together into **The Now**.

Other meditations that follow will provide more in-depth guidance about healing past issues or preparing for upcoming events, but it's important to understand that, regardless of the timeframe, several issues may be covered during the same meditation.

Meditation: Healing the Present

Find a comfortable and very quiet place to sit, a spot where you won't be disturbed by people talking, telephones ringing, TV or music playing, or other interruptions.

Remove your shoes, and loosen any clothing that feels too tight.

If you're sitting on the ground in an attitude of contemplation, be sure to keep your back straight. If this is difficult for you to do, sit against a wall for support.

If you're sitting on a chair or on a sofa, let your back be supported by the furniture. Your feet should be resting, uncrossed, flat on the ground.

Place your hands on your lap, palms up, with the fingers of one hand resting on top of the fingers of the other hand, and the tips of your thumbs gently touching, forming a circle.

Close your eyes and become conscious of your breathing. Breathe deeply at first with your mouth closed, inhaling only through your nose. Then with your mouth slightly open, exhale slowly. Hear the soft whoosh of air as you're exhaling it out. Do this seven times.

With each inhaled breath of pure, refreshing air, feel yourself becoming calmer. As you exhale, release any random thoughts and any tension you've acquired during the day. Let your body become more and more deeply relaxed with every breath, in and out.

To deepen your relaxation, begin at the top of your head. Become aware of each part of your face as the tension drifts away, and your facial muscles become more relaxed . . . in your forehead . . . eyebrow area . . . eyelids . . . eyes . . . cheeks . . . jaw . . . and lips.

Your facial muscles are now so relaxed that you may even feel yourself smiling.

Let your tongue roll upward and gently rest on the roof of your mouth, forming a circle inside of your body to correspond to the circle you formed with your hands on the outside of your body.

Become aware of the tension being released from your neck . . . shoulders . . . arms . . . and hands. You should feel your shoulders drop slightly as the tension drifts away. Feel the sense of calming relaxation flow all the way down your arms, through your hands, and out to your fingertips.

Let your breathing naturally become more shallow and rhythmic.

Become aware of the relaxation flowing gently through the main part of your body . . . through the areas of your chest and upper back . . . your abdomen and lower back . . . through your hips and buttocks . . . and thighs.

Let it continue flowing down through your lower legs . . . through your feet . . . and all the way to the tips of your toes.

Continue to breathe at a naturally slower and more relaxed pace as you experience a wonderful sense of total relaxation.

If your mind wanders, calmly bring yourself back by focusing your attention on the gentle rhythm of your breathing.

Next, visualize that, from the soles of your feet, you're extending strong roots deep down into Mother Earth. Just as a wise old tree does, these roots burrow deep into the ground beneath your feet and spread out to find nourishment and water, the symbol of life energy.

With your third eye (your spiritual eye, located between your eyebrows), *look upward. See a wonderful, shimmering white light coming down from the heavens straight to you. It's the light of the Universe. It's the all-knowing, all-seeing light and it's here for you, for your benefit and the benefit of your pets. In it is all the wisdom you need to have available to you at this moment.*

Feel the warmth of this loving energy as it gently enters through the top of your head and fills your entire being all the way to the tips of your toes. So much loving light flows through you that what you cannot hold overflows from the top of your head like a fountain. Your entire body, inside and out, is now bathed in this loving light.

This stream of light energy will continue to flow through and around you during your entire meditation to envelop you, both inside and out, in it's loving, healing care. You're very relaxed, and feeling very nurtured.

Breathe gently as you take a few moments to let yourself totally experience all the loving tenderness of the healing light of the Universe.

Now envision yourself in a tranquil garden setting. Flowers, plants and bushes of every variety create a feast for the eyes and spirit. Colors of every shade and hue, both soft and vibrant, fill you with a sense of peace and joy. Fragrances waft on the gentle breeze, while the sun sparkles through the trees. This is **The Present Moment.** *Allow yourself some precious time to let its beauty permeate all of your senses.*

As beautiful as everything is, though, you're eager to follow the tree-lined path you see at the far side of the garden. It, too, is abundant with natural beauty.

Notice the firm support of the earth under your feet as you're walking.

Feel the gentle breeze as it touches your face and arms.

Observe the vibrant colors of all the bushes and flowers you see along the way. Smell their delightful fragrances. Notice the shapes and sizes of any rocks and stones, and feel the smoothness or roughness of their textures. Hear the clean, clear, fresh water running in a nearby brook or stream.

Feel yourself being the joyful, balanced, well grounded person you truly are at the very center of your being.

Allow yourself to experience your gifts of inner beauty, inner strength, and inner wisdom.

Know that in your spirit you're a beautiful reflection of the One who created you.

As you approach the end of this path, you discover that it's led you right into one of your favorite places where you like to spend time. This may be a place in nature like a park, an out of the way mountain top, a far away island with a majestic waterfall, near a river where you enjoy watching the rapids, at a secluded beach, or any other place of beauty and serenity. It may also be a make-believe place which no one else has ever seen, like a space healing station located somewhere in the universe.

Whatever place you choose, it's always one where you feel very safe and secure, and just being there calms your spirit, or sends it soaring with joy. This is the place we call **The Now.**

Find a comfortable place to sit and allow yourself time to absorb every detail in all of the beauty that surrounds you. Notice the light . . . the colors . . . the fragrances . . . the sounds . . . the sizes . . . the shapes . . . the textures. Look . . . listen . . . touch . . . enjoy. Let yourself become intimately familiar with everything about your special place.

Notice also that there's a bridge to your left, and another bridge to your right. They're always available in case you need to help your pet with either a past problem or a future event.

As you bask in this beautiful paradise, remember that this is your safe place. You may come here anytime you need to relax. No one else is allowed here unless you offer a special invitation.

Quietly remain in **The Now** *enjoying the peace and tranquility for as long as you wish.*

Then when you're ready, picture your pet in your mind and call her by name. Ask her to come and spend some spiritual time with you.

Greet her as you normally would, telling her how much you love her. Send your love to her as a ray of light from your heart to hers.

Tell her you wanted to meet her in this special place because you'd like to help her heal physically, emotionally, spiritually, or behaviorally from something that's bothering her.

Tell her, in clear detail, what you've been noticing, and that you'd like to do anything you can to help her feel better.

If **physical healing** *is needed, then in your mind's eye, visualize yourself placing your hands over the affected area of your pet's body, while sending the loving intention of healing* *to her. See the light, which is lovingly enveloping your own body inside and out, flowing through the palms of your hands as you place them, in your mind's eye, wherever your animal is hurt or sick.*

The stream of light will be constant, and although it's applied to a specific area, very soon it will engulf your pet's entire body as it travels anywhere it's needed. You never have to worry about depleting the amount of healing light you have because it's coming from an infinite Source to whom you're always connected.

*If **emotional healing** is needed, talk with your pet as if you were talking to another person, explaining what you've observed and why you'd like to help her heal this particular problem.*

In your mind's eye, touch her heart with the palms of your hands and see the light gently enter her heart and flow throughout the inside of her body. Ask the healing light of the Universe to make her emotionally well again. Assure your pet that you'll help her in any way you can.

*If **spiritual healing** is needed, again talk with her explaining everything just as you would to another human. Send the healing light to your pet so that it not only encompasses her physical body, but also all of her auras. Tell her you'll make every effort to help her live a life free from stress and discomfort.*

*If **behavioral healing** is needed, be very positive in the way you express to your pet what she needs to do. Refrain from telling her what you don't want her to do. Instead, describe the way you do want her to act whenever she'd be doing it just right.*

Ask her if she knows what kind of help would be best for her.

(If you've discovered a reason to visit **The Past** or **The Future** during this same meditation, take a moment to cross either the bridge to your left or the bridge to your right and spend some time there as you look for the original cause of a current behavior problem, or explain something about the future to your pet.)

Remember that the healing light of the Universe is still flowing through you. Know that the Universe sends out only love and goodness, and that It's absolutely unlimited in Its ability to care for each being It has created.

At the end of your conversation with your pet in **The Now***, (or when you've come back to* **The Now** *from* **The Past** *or* **The Future***), spend a little more quiet, loving time together.*

Ask her if there's anything else she wants to tell you, or if there's anything she needs to have you do for her.

Then spend a few more moments of quiet, loving time with your pet, simply allowing yourselves some time to be together in the silence. Sometimes, it's in the stillness that something important will be shared.

When you know you're both finished, thank her for these moments of spiritual closeness and send her on her way, knowing that the energy of the Universe continues to do its loving, healing work in her. You'll either see her walk away or simply disappear.

Spend a few additional quiet, peaceful moments in **The Now** *by yourself. Know that you can return any time you want, and that the joy and beauty you've experienced will always be here for you.*

It's then time to say farewell to your special place of peace and serenity in **The Now** *and prepare to return to* **The Present Moment** *in the tranquil garden, so begin walking back along the path that originally brought you here.*

Continue to experience all of the vibrant colors, fragrant scents, and beautiful sights. Notice again the textures, shapes and sizes of the rocks and stones you observed when you first walked this path . . . hear the sound of the water in the brook or stream fading more and more softly into the distance.

Follow the path until you arrive back in the peaceful garden where you began this journey. Enjoy the beauty once again, but only for a few moments this time, because you're now ready to return to your normal state of awareness.

Feel yourself in your sitting position once again. Let the roots you put down into Mother Earth recede back into the soles of your feet. Visualize how they're absorbed perfectly back inside of your body as they become smaller and smaller. Wiggle your toes and become even more consciously aware of your body.

Give thanks for the beautiful healing energy that surrounds and permeates every part of your being. Then let it travel upward and exit through the top of your head. See how it blends into the heavens and know that it will always be there for you anytime you need it.

Now become completely aware of your physical body and the present time. Stretch luxuriously, feeling rested and joyful.

Breathe deeply and give thanks.

If necessary, count from one to five, becoming much more alert, aware, and physically active with each successive number . . . and when you're ready, open your eyes.

Chapter 13

Guided Meditation 4

Healing The Past

You'll use this meditation when you know you need to help your pet resolve a problem which has its roots somewhere in her past.

If your pet is presently terrified or overly agitated by an object or a recurring event, like the noise of a vacuum cleaner, a trip to the groomer, or the sound of a garbage truck, it may be that something happened to her in either the recent or more distant past, and she's reacting to the memory of it now.

In the case of an older adopted pet, you may currently be seeing behavior issues that are the direct result of neglect or some trauma that happened in her life before she ever came to live with you.

This might have had something to do with physical or emotional abuse, people she feared or didn't like, noisy children, aggressive animals, difficult conditions she lived in, excessive punishment even when she didn't do anything wrong, or anything else that might have upset her.

In this type of meditation, it will be very important to listen with special care to whatever your pet may have to tell you.

But what if you feel you aren't receiving any helpful information? To the beginner, it may sometimes seem as if little or no information is forthcoming. You may be expecting to clearly hear a voice, or see a detailed videotape of what happened, or receive definite ideas about what you should be doing to help her. But sometimes the feelings or pictures your pet sends are so subtle that you may think nothing's happening.

This isn't true. Please know that even if you feel **you** aren't receiving anything, your pet most likely **is** receiving pictures from you. Our thoughts and feelings are easy for pets to read, so while the sharing of information might seem one sided for the moment, in time, and with practice, you too will be able to receive information.

When you seem to be having difficulty seeing, hearing or feeling anything, wait quietly as long as you can maintain your focus. That means not letting any other thoughts wander into your mind. When or if they do, it means that you haven't yet reached a deep enough level of meditation necessary to experience these new feelings, sensations and images.

Simply let it go and don't be concerned about it for now. Just know that with practice and patience it will happen.

Again, your pet will no doubt understand the concerns you've shared with her, and you'll soon see that there will be a slight difference, not only in how your pet approaches the problem, but also in how you see it.

Meditation: Healing The Past

Find a comfortable and very quiet place to sit, a spot where you won't be disturbed by people talking, telephones ringing, TV or music playing, or other interruptions.

Remove your shoes, and loosen any clothing that feels too tight.

If you're sitting on the ground in an attitude of contemplation, be sure to keep your back straight. If this is difficult for you to do, sit against a wall for support.

If you're sitting on a chair or on a sofa, let your back be supported by the furniture. Your feet should be resting, uncrossed, flat on the ground.

Place your hands on your lap, palms up, with the fingers of one hand resting on top of the fingers of the other hand, and the tips of your thumbs gently touching, forming a circle.

Close your eyes and become conscious of your breathing. Breathe deeply at first with your mouth closed, inhaling only through your nose. Then with your mouth slightly open, exhale slowly. Hear the soft whoosh of air as you're exhaling it out. Do this seven times.

With each inhaled breath of pure, refreshing air, feel yourself becoming calmer. As you exhale, release any random thoughts and any tension you've acquired during the day. Let your body become more and more deeply relaxed with every breath, in and out.

To deepen your relaxation, begin at the top of your head. Become aware of each part of your face as the tension drifts away and your facial muscles become more relaxed . . . in your forehead . . . eyebrow area . . . eyelids . . . eyes . . . cheeks . . . jaw . . . and lips.

Your facial muscles are now so relaxed that you may even feel yourself smiling.

Let your tongue roll upward and gently rest on the roof of your mouth, forming a circle inside of your body to correspond to the circle you formed with your hands on the outside of your body.

Become aware of the tension being released from your neck . . . shoulders . . . arms . . . and hands. You should feel your shoulders drop slightly as the tension drifts away. Feel the sense of calming relaxation flow all the way down your arms, through your hands, and out to your fingertips.

Let your breathing naturally become more shallow and rhythmic.

Become aware of the relaxation flowing gently through the main part of your body . . . through the areas of your chest and upper back . . . your abdomen and lower back . . . through your hips and buttocks . . . and thighs.

Let it continue flowing down through your lower legs . . . through your feet . . . and all the way to the tips of your toes.

Continue to breathe at a naturally slower and more relaxed pace as you experience a wonderful sense of total relaxation.

If your mind wanders, calmly bring yourself back by focusing your attention on the gentle rhythm of your breathing.

Now, visualize that, from the soles of your feet, you're extending strong roots deep down into Mother Earth. Just as a wise old tree does, these roots burrow deep into the ground beneath your feet and spread out to find nourishment and water, the symbol of life energy.

With your third eye (your spiritual eye, located between your eyebrows), *look upward. See a wonderful, shimmering white light coming down from the heavens straight to you. It's the light of the Universe. It's the all-knowing, all-seeing light and it's here for you, for your benefit and the benefit of your pets. In it is all the wisdom you need to have available to you at this moment.*

Feel the warmth of this loving energy as it gently enters through the top of your head and fills your entire being all the way to the tips of your toes. So much loving light flows through you that what you cannot hold overflows from the top of your head like a fountain. Your entire body, inside and out, is now bathed in this loving light.

This stream of light energy will continue to flow through and around you during your entire meditation to envelop you, both inside and out, in it's loving, healing care. You're very relaxed, and feeling very nurtured.

Breathe gently as you take a few moments to let yourself totally experience all the loving tenderness of the healing light of the Universe.

Now envision yourself in a tranquil garden setting. Flowers, plants and bushes of every variety create a feast for the eyes and spirit. Colors of every shade and hue, both soft and vibrant, fill you with a sense of peace and joy. Fragrances waft on the gentle breeze, while the sun sparkles through the trees. This is **The Present Moment.** *Allow yourself some precious time to let its beauty permeate all of your senses.*

As beautiful as everything is, though, you're eager to follow the tree-lined path you see at the far side of the garden. It, too, is abundant with natural beauty.

Notice the firm support of the earth under your feet as you're walking.

Feel the gentle breeze as it touches your face and arms.

Observe the vibrant colors of all the bushes and flowers you see along the way. Smell their delightful fragrances. Notice the shapes and sizes of any rocks and stones, and feel the smoothness or roughness of their textures. Hear the clean, clear, fresh water running in a nearby brook or stream.

Feel yourself being the joyful, balanced, well grounded person you truly are at the very center of your being.

Allow yourself to experience your gifts of inner beauty, inner strength, and inner wisdom.

Know that in your spirit you're a beautiful reflection of the One who created you.

As you approach the end of this path, you discover that it's led you right into one of your favorite places where you like to spend time. This may be a place in nature like a park, an out of the way mountain top, a far away island with a majestic waterfall, near a river where you enjoy watching the rapids, at a secluded beach, or any other place of beauty and serenity. It may also be a make-believe place which no one else has ever seen, like a space healing station located somewhere in the universe.

Whatever place you choose, it's always one where you feel very safe and secure, and just being there calms your spirit, or sends it soaring with joy. This is the place we call **The Now.**

Find a comfortable place to sit and allow yourself time to absorb every detail in all of the beauty that surrounds you. Notice the light . . . the colors . . . the fragrances . . . the sounds . . . the sizes . . . the shapes . . . the textures. Look . . . listen . . . touch . . . enjoy. Let yourself become intimately familiar with everything about your special place.

Notice also that there's a bridge to your left, and another bridge to your right. Soon, you'll cross the bridge to the left because you want to help your pet heal a problem which has its origin in the near or distant past.

As you bask in this beautiful paradise, remember that this is your safe place. You may come here anytime you need to relax. No one else is allowed here unless you offer a special invitation.

Quietly remain in **The Now** *enjoying the peace and tranquility of this special place for as long as you wish.*

When you're ready, picture your animal friend in your mind and call her by name. Ask her to come and spend some spiritual time with you.

Greet her as you normally would, telling her how much you love her. Send your love to her as a ray of light from your heart to hers.

Tell her you wanted to meet her in this special place because you'd like to help her heal physically, emotionally, spiritually, or behaviorally from whatever's bothering her.

Enjoy a few quiet moments together in **The Now.**

Then, since you know you need to heal something that has its roots in your pet's past, walk together toward the bridge on your left. Pay close attention to everything around you in **The Now** *as you go. Smell the fragrances in the air . . . observe the wide variety of colors . . . reach out and touch anything you wish so that you can feel its texture. Experience everything with all of your senses.*

As you cross the bridge together, you feel a peaceful sense of walking back in time.

(This new location can be a completely different area of your favorite place, or it can be any other special place of your choosing. The important thing is that by crossing the bridge to **The Past**, you'll both have the sense that you're now taking a walk back in time.)

Enjoy a few moments as you let each one of your senses become fully aware of the beautiful surroundings in which you now find yourself on the other side of the bridge. Let the sights, sounds and textures of it permeate all of your senses.

While both of you are in **The Past**, *walk slowly or sit quietly in the silence.*

Tell your pet exactly what it is you'd like to talk to her about. Let her know that you love her so much that you'd like to help her heal from something that took place in her past, but in order to do that, you need to better understand what it was that happened to her in an earlier part of her life.

Ask her to share with you some images from her past, or to tell you about any unpleasant things she previously experienced which might be causing her to have a problem now.

Let your mind relax as you wait for some kind of communication: a picture, a feeling, a smell or a taste sensation that she sends you. Pay special attention to anything you feel in your own body, or see or hear in your mind's eye. Your pet may tell you something that will help you understand her previous experiences.

(If the information you receive is something you wouldn't have thought of on your own, then it's no doubt definitely something your pet is telling you.)

If your pet is willing to share specific information with you about events in her past history, then you'll be able to help her understand what she needs to know so that she can change her perception about the present.

If you're able to receive some help from her, thank her and tell her that you now have a much better understanding of her situation.

Ask her if she knows what she can do to be an active participant in her own healing.

Can she tell you what you can do to help her make changes in her behavior?

If what she wants you to do isn't reasonable, ask her if she'd be willing to compromise and take somewhat of a middle road.

If you know what she can do, be specific. Give her some examples and let her choose the best solution.

If she doesn't seem to want to share any specific details at all, ask her in more general terms if she at least remembers anything happening in her past that's now causing the way she feels about something in the present. Then try asking her some specific questions pertaining to her past, and listen for her answers.

Give her lots of reassurance and support. Let her know that what happened previously belonged only to that time, and that her life now is meant to be free from any problems she may have had in the past.

Tell her that her home is now with you, and you'll provide her with everything she needs to make her comfortable. Her life with you will be very different from her unpleasant past experiences, because her life from now on will be filled with your love and tender care. Maybe all she needs is reassurance that her home with you is her permanent home, and you'll always provide her with the love and care she needs.

Remember that the healing light of the Universe is still flowing through you. Let that healing light energy, which is flowing through your own body, also be directed to your pet to help her heal from any past traumas. Know that the Universe sends out only love and goodness, and that It's absolutely unlimited in Its ability to care for each being It has created.

Also know that your love, and the love of the Universe, is motivating your pet to release her past experiences, and look at those in her present life in a new and healing way.

Thank your pet for listening to what you had to say and reassure her that you'll still do all you can to help her understand that she's now safe and secure with you, and that she can release all of her past fears and worries.

When you're both finished, walk together from **The Past** *back over the bridge into* **The Now***.*

When you're comfortably settled in **The Now** *once again, ask your pet if there's anything else she wants to tell you, or if there's anything she needs to have you do for her.*

Then spend a few more moments of quiet, loving time with your pet, simply allowing yourselves some time to be together in the silence. Sometimes, it's in the stillness that something important will be shared.

When both of you are completely finished, thank her for these moments of spiritual closeness and send her on her way, knowing that the energy of the Universe continues to do its loving, healing work in her. You may see her walk away, or she may simply disappear.

Spend a few additional quiet, peaceful moments in **The Now** *by yourself. Know that you can return any time you* *want, and that the joy and beauty you've experienced will always be here for you.*

It's then time to say farewell to your special place of peace and serenity in **The Now** *and prepare to return to* **The Present Moment** *in the tranquil garden, so begin walking back along the path that originally brought you here.*

Continue to experience all of the vibrant colors, fragrant scents, and beautiful sights. Notice again the textures, shapes and sizes of the rocks and stones you observed when you first walked this path . . . hear the sound of the water in the brook or stream fading more and more softly into the distance.

Follow the path until you arrive back in the peaceful garden where you began this journey. Enjoy the beauty once again, but only for a few moments this time, because you're now ready to return to your normal state of awareness.

Feel yourself in your sitting position once again. Let the roots you put down into Mother Earth recede back into the soles of your feet. Visualize how they're absorbed perfectly back inside of your body as they become smaller and smaller. Wiggle your toes and become even more consciously aware of your body.

Give thanks for the beautiful healing energy that surrounds and permeates every part of your being. Then let it travel upward and exit through the top of your head. See how it blends into the heavens and know that it will always be there for you anytime you need it.

Now become completely aware of your physical body and the present time. Stretch luxuriously, feeling rested and joyful.

Breathe deeply and give thanks.

If necessary, count from one to five, becoming much more alert, aware, and physically active with each successive number. When you're ready, open your eyes.

Chapter 14

Guided Meditation 5

Preparing for a Future Event

You'll use this meditation when you need to tell your pet about something that's going to be happening, like an upcoming vacation, a move to another house, spending time at a boarding facility, or whenever someone new is about to become part of the family -- a different roommate, another pet, or a new baby.

If you're soon going to be starting a special activity like basic behavior training, even for a young puppy, while the two of you are in **The Future**, send a picture to your pet showing him where you'll be going, how you'll get there, who else will be there, how proud you'll be when he learns each new behavior, how you'll come back home again, and how you'll practice together many times until he can do each new behavior easily on cue.

You may also need to prepare your pet when a family member is going to be leaving home to live elsewhere. This is a helpful thing to do if a son or daughter is going away to college, or when only one member of the family will be moving to another location. In this case, you may even want to ask your pet to decide which person he'd like to continue to live with, or you may need to help him cope with the sense of loss he'll feel when the other person does move out.

And, when your pet's going to be separated from a beloved pet companion in the near future—for any reason, including illness, death, or boarding at the vets or at a vacation kennel—if you'll just take time to cross the bridge to **The Future** to talk with him, you'll be better able to prepare him to understand and accept what's going to be happening.

It's very important for your pet to receive clear visual pictures from you showing him what his future will be like, so be very creative and detailed whenever you talk with him.

In each case, it's also important to ask your pet what you can do to make the upcoming changes easier for him.

But what if you aren't sure the information you're sending is being received by your pet? This probably isn't true. Our thoughts and feelings are very easy for pets to read, so just know that even if the sharing of information feels new to you, your pet will understand what you've told him, as long as you've created clear and detailed pictures.

You'll also want to ask your pet to tell you his feelings about what you've told him. If you seem to be having difficulty seeing, hearing or feeling anything in response from him, wait quietly as long as you can maintain your focus. That means not letting any other thoughts wander into your mind. When or if they do, it means that you haven't yet reached a deep enough level of meditation necessary to experience receiving information from your pet. Simply let it go, and don't be concerned about it for now. Just know that with practice and patience it will happen.

Meditation: Healing The Future

Find a comfortable and very quiet place to sit, a spot where you won't be disturbed by people talking, telephones ringing, TV or music playing, or other interruptions.

Remove your shoes, and loosen any clothing that feels too tight.

If you're sitting on the ground in an attitude of contemplation, be sure to keep your back straight. If this is difficult for you to do, sit against a wall for support.

If you're sitting on a chair or on a sofa, let your back be supported by the furniture. Your feet should be resting, uncrossed, flat on the ground.

Place your hands on your lap, palms up, with the fingers of one hand resting on top of the fingers of the other hand, and the tips of your thumbs gently touching, forming a circle.

Close your eyes and become conscious of your breathing. Breathe deeply at first with your mouth closed, inhaling only through your nose. Then with your mouth slightly open, exhale slowly. Hear the soft whoosh of air as you're exhaling it out. Do this seven times.

With each inhaled breath of pure, refreshing air, feel yourself becoming calmer. As you exhale, release any random thoughts and any tension you've acquired during the day. Let your body become more and more deeply relaxed with every breath, in and out.

To deepen your relaxation, begin at the top of your head. Become aware of each part of your face as the tension drifts away and your facial muscles become more relaxed . . . in your forehead . . . eyebrow area . . . eyelids . . . eyes . . . cheeks . . . jaw . . . and lips.

Your facial muscles are now so relaxed that you may even feel yourself smiling.

Let your tongue roll upward and gently rest on the roof of your mouth, forming a circle inside of your body to correspond to the circle you formed with your hands on the outside of your body.

Become aware of the tension being released from your neck . . . shoulders . . . arms . . . and hands. You should feel your shoulders drop slightly as the tension drifts away. Feel the sense of calming relaxation flow all the way down your arms, through your hands, and out to your fingertips.

Let your breathing naturally become more shallow and rhythmic.

Become aware of the relaxation flowing gently through the main part of your body . . . through the areas of your chest and upper back . . . your abdomen and lower back . . . through your hips and buttocks . . . and thighs.

Let it continue flowing down through your lower legs . . . through your feet . . . and all the way to the tips of your toes.

Continue to breathe at a naturally slower and more relaxed pace as you experience a wonderful sense of total relaxation.

If your mind wanders, calmly bring yourself back by focusing your attention on the gentle rhythm of your breathing.

Now, visualize that, from the soles of your feet, you're extending strong roots deep down into Mother Earth. Just as a wise old tree does, these roots burrow deep into the ground beneath your feet and spread out to find nourishment and water, the symbol of life energy.

With your third eye (your spiritual eye, located between your eyebrows), look upward. See a wonderful, shimmering white light coming down from the heavens straight to you. It's the light of the Universe. It's the all-knowing, all-seeing light and it's here for you, for your benefit and the benefit of your pets. In it is all the wisdom you need to have available to you at this moment.

Feel the warmth of this loving energy as it gently enters through the top of your head and fills your entire being all the way to the tips of your toes. So much loving light flows through you that what you cannot hold overflows from the top of your head like a fountain. Your entire body, inside and out, is now bathed in this loving light.

This stream of light energy will continue to flow through and around you during your entire meditation to envelop you, both inside and out, in it's loving, healing care. You're very relaxed, and feeling very nurtured.

Breathe gently as you take a few moments to let yourself totally experience all the loving tenderness of the healing light of the Universe.

Now envision yourself in a tranquil garden setting. Flowers, plants and bushes of every variety create a feast for the eyes and spirit. Colors of every shade and hue, both soft and vibrant, fill you with a sense of peace and joy. Fragrances waft on the gentle breeze, while the sun sparkles through the trees. This is **The Present Moment.** *Allow yourself some precious time to let its beauty permeate all of your senses.*

As beautiful as everything is, though, you're eager to follow the tree-lined path you see at the far side of the garden. It, too, is abundant with natural beauty.

Notice the firm support of the earth under your feet as you're walking.

Feel the gentle breeze as it touches your face and arms.

Observe the vibrant colors of all the bushes and flowers you see along the way. Smell their delightful fragrances. Notice the shapes and sizes of any rocks and stones, and feel the smoothness or roughness of their textures. Hear the clean, clear, fresh water running in a nearby brook or stream.

Feel yourself being the joyful, balanced, well grounded person you truly are at the very center of your being.

Allow yourself to experience your gifts of inner beauty, inner strength, and inner wisdom.

Know that in your spirit you're a beautiful reflection of the One who created you.

As you approach the end of this path, you discover that it's led you right into one of your favorite places where you like to spend time. This may be a place in nature like a park, an out of the way mountain top, a far away island with a majestic waterfall, near a river where you enjoy watching the rapids, at a secluded beach, or any other place of beauty and serenity. It may also be a make-believe place which no one else has ever seen, like a space healing station located somewhere in the universe.

Whatever place you choose, it's always one where you feel very safe and secure, and just being there calms your spirit, or sends it soaring with joy. This is the place we call **The Now.**

Find a comfortable place to sit and allow yourself time to absorb every detail in all of the beauty that surrounds you. Notice the light . . . the colors . . . the fragrances . . . the sounds . . . the sizes . . . the shapes . . . the textures. Look . . . listen . . . touch . . . enjoy. Let yourself become intimately familiar with everything about your special place.

Notice also that there's a bridge to your left, and another bridge to your right. Soon, you'll cross the bridge to the right because you want to talk to your pet about something new that will be happening in the near future.

As you bask in this beautiful paradise, remember that this is your safe place. You may come here anytime you need to relax. No one else is allowed here unless you offer a special invitation.

Quietly remain in **The Now** *enjoying the peace and tranquility of this special place for as long as you wish.*

When you're ready, picture your pet in your mind and call him by name. Ask him to come and spend some spiritual time with you.

Greet him as you normally would, telling him how much you love him. Send your love to him as a ray of light from your heart to his.

Tell him you wanted to meet him in this special place because you'd like to help him understand something new and different that will soon be happening in his life.

Enjoy a few quiet moments together in **The Now**.

Then, since you know you need to talk to your pet about something that will be happening soon, walk together toward the bridge on your right. Pay close attention to everything around you in **The Now** *as you go. Smell the fragrances in the air . . . observe the wide variety of colors . . . reach out and touch anything you wish so that you can feel its texture. Experience everything with all of your senses.*

As you cross the bridge together, you feel a peaceful sense of walking forward in time.

(This new location can be a different part of your favorite place, or you may even decide to select an entirely new location altogether -- one which also has special significance for you. The important thing is that by crossing the bridge to **The Future**, you'll both have the sense that you're now taking a walk forward in time.)

Take a moment to let each one of your senses become fully aware of the beautiful surroundings in which you now find yourself on the other side of the bridge. Let the sights, sounds and textures of it permeate all of your senses.

While both of you are in **The Future**, *walk together slowly or sit quietly in the silence.*

Tell your pet exactly what you want him to know about the upcoming change. Create detailed pictures in your mind about the people, places and differences in daily routines that may become a part of what's going to be new.

(If you're not exactly sure how things will look, for instance at a new house, try at least to convey the important qualities that will still be part of your pet's life -- like love, affection, having his needs met, enjoying meals, treats, walks and time outdoors.)

Give him lots of reassurance and support. Be sure to tell him that you'll love him just as much as you always have, and that his needs will always be taken care of. This is particularly important if a new baby or a new spouse is about to join the family.

Again, be very specific when you're talking to him.

Ask him if he has any questions, and listen for his answers. Try to answer his questions as best as you can with whatever information you do have.

If you know what he can do, be specific.

(Will he need to wait quietly nearby while you care for a new baby? Should he stay out of the new roommate's bedroom? If you're going on vacation, tell him you've provided for his care and that he, too, should have fun while you're away and wait patiently for you to return. If it's a move to a new house, will you need to have him wait in the yard at the old house until all of the furniture has been put into the moving van? How will he be traveling from one place to the other? When he arrives at his new house are there any places that will be off limits for a while? Where in his new home will he be free to go?)

Now that you've told him all about the upcoming changes, ask him how he feels about them.

Ask him if he knows what he can do to be an active participant in what's going to be happening.

Ask your pet if there's anything you can do to make the transition easier for him.

After each question, listen attentively for his answer.

Provide him with plenty of assurance and support, reminding him that he can always count on you to love and care for him.

Let the light of the healing energy, which is flowing through your own body, also be directed to your pet to help strengthen and prepare him to accept the changes that will be taking place.

Know that your love, and the love of the Universe, is motivating him to understand his new circumstances and adapt easily to them.

When you're satisfied that you've clearly communicated this new information to your pet about what's going to be happening soon, thank him for listening and for helping with the changes. Then walk together across the bridge from **The Future** *back into* **The Now.**

When you're comfortably settled in **The Now** *once again, ask your pet if there's anything else he wants to tell you, or if there's anything he needs to have you do for him.*

Then spend a few more moments of quiet, loving time with your pet, simply allowing yourselves some time to be together in the silence. Sometimes, it's in the stillness that something important will be shared.

Next, thank him for these moments of spiritual closeness and then send him on his way, knowing that the energy of the Universe continues to do its loving, healing work in him, preparing him for the changes that are to come. You may see him walking away, or he may simply disappear.

Spend a few additional quiet, peaceful moments in **The Now** *by yourself. Know that you can return any time you want, and that the joy and beauty you've experienced will always be here for you.*

It's then time to say farewell to your special place of peace and serenity in **The Now** *and prepare to return to* **The Present Moment** *in the tranquil garden, so begin walking back along the path that originally brought you here.*

Continue to experience all of the vibrant colors, fragrant scents, and beautiful sights. Notice again the textures, shapes and sizes of the rocks and stones you observed when you first walked this path . . . hear the sound of the water in the brook or stream fading more and more softly into the distance.

Follow the path until you arrive back in the peaceful garden where you began this journey. Enjoy the beauty once again, but only for a few moments this time, because you're now ready to return to your normal state of awareness.

Feel yourself in your sitting position once again. Let the roots you put down into Mother Earth recede back into the soles of your feet. Visualize how they're absorbed perfectly back inside of your body as they become smaller and smaller. Wiggle your toes and become even more consciously aware of your body.

Give thanks for the beautiful healing energy that surrounds and permeates every part of your being. Then let it travel upward and exit through the top of your head. See how it blends into the heavens and know that it will always be there for you anytime you need it.

Now become completely aware of your physical body and the present time. Stretch luxuriously, feeling rested and joyful.

Breathe deeply and give thanks.

If necessary, count from one to five, becoming much more alert, aware, and physically active with each successive number . . . and when you're ready, open your eyes.

Chapter 15

Guided Meditation 6

Talking with a Pet in Spirit

You'll use this meditation when you want to talk to your pets who have already made their transitions back into Spirit, no matter how long ago they may have left their physical bodies.

Before you try to visit with them, however, it's wisest to wait at least a month or so after they pass on. This gives them the necessary time they may need to become completely readjusted to being in Spirit once again.

When you do talk with them, you can use your time together to find out where they are, who they're with, and what they're doing.

You may also want to inquire about exactly what caused them to make their transitions, if you don't already know. They may, or may not, be willing to share this information with you. Many pets who are already in Spirit sometimes don't feel the need to talk about past events from their previous experiences, or they prefer not to do so. Where they are now is so beautiful and peaceful, they no longer want to think about anything that happened in the past, especially if it was difficult or painful.

If necessary, this visit can be a wonderful time, too, for you to ask forgiveness for things you did, or didn't do, or wish you'd done, so that you can give yourself some much needed closure.

You may also want to ask your pets in Spirit if they ever come to visit you regularly or occasionally, or if they'll ever be coming back to you in another body. You might even want to ask if they can send you another animal friend to fill the current void in your life, especially if they aren't planning to return again themselves.

If you presently have a pet who's dying, you may also want to use this bridge to talk with a former pet, or with an angel, who might help your present animal make an easier transition to the other side when his or her time comes.

Once you've spoken with a former pet, who has reassured you of his or her continual love for you, you'll then know that there really is no such thing as death. Although their physical bodies are no longer here with us, their spirits still love and remain with us forever.

Meditation: Talking with a Pet in Spirit

Find a comfortable and very quiet place to sit, a spot where you won't be disturbed by people talking, telephones ringing, TV or music playing, or other interruptions.

Remove your shoes, and loosen any clothing that feels too tight.

If you're sitting on the ground in an attitude of contemplation, be sure to keep your back straight. If this is difficult for you to do, sit against a wall for support.

If you're sitting on a chair or on a sofa, let your back be supported by the furniture. Your feet should be resting, uncrossed, flat on the ground.

Place your hands on your lap, palms up, with the fingers of one hand resting on top of the fingers of the other hand, and the tips of your thumbs gently touching, forming a circle.

Close your eyes and become conscious of your breathing. Breathe deeply at first with your mouth closed, inhaling only through your nose. Then with your mouth slightly open, exhale slowly. Hear the soft whoosh of air as you're exhaling it out. Do this seven times.

With each inhaled breath of pure, refreshing air, feel yourself becoming calmer. As you exhale, release any random thoughts and any tension you've acquired during the day. Let your body become more and more deeply relaxed with every breath, in and out.

To deepen your relaxation, begin at the top of your head. Become aware of each part of your face as the tension drifts away and your facial muscles become more relaxed . . . in your forehead . . . eyebrow area . . . eyelids . . . eyes . . . cheeks . . . jaw . . . and lips.

Your facial muscles are now so relaxed that you may even feel yourself smiling.

Let your tongue roll upward and gently rest on the roof of your mouth, forming a circle inside of your body to correspond to the circle you formed with your hands on the outside of your body.

Become aware of the tension being released from your neck and shoulders . . . arms . . . and hands. You should feel your shoulders drop slightly as the tension drifts away. Feel the sense of calming relaxation flow all the way down your arms, through your hands, and out to your fingertips.

Let your breathing naturally become more shallow and rhythmic.

Become aware of the relaxation flowing gently through the main part of your body . . . through the areas of your chest and upper back . . . your abdomen and lower back . . . now through your hips . . . buttocks . . . and thighs.

Let it continue flowing down through your lower legs . . . through your feet . . . and all the way to the tips of your toes.

Continue to breathe at a naturally slower and more relaxed pace as you experience a wonderful sense of total relaxation.

If your mind wanders, calmly bring yourself back by focusing your attention on the gentle rhythm of your breathing.

Now, visualize that, from the soles of your feet, you're extending strong roots deep down into Mother Earth. Just as a wise old tree does, these roots burrow deep into the ground beneath your feet and spread out to find nourishment and water, the symbol of life energy.

With your third eye (your spiritual eye, located between your eyebrows), *look upward. See a wonderful, shimmering white light coming down from the heavens straight to you. It's the light of the Universe. It's the all-knowing, all-seeing light and it's here for you, for your benefit and the benefit of your pets. In it is all the wisdom you need to have available to you at this moment.*

Feel the warmth of this loving energy as it gently enters through the top of your head and fills your entire being all the way to the tips of your toes. So much loving light flows through you that what you cannot hold overflows from the top of your head like a fountain. Your entire body, inside and out, is now bathed in this loving light.

This stream of light energy will continue to flow through and around you during your entire meditation to envelop you, both inside and out, in it's loving, healing care. You're very relaxed, and feeling very nurtured.

Breathe gently as you take a few moments to let yourself totally experience all the loving tenderness of the healing light of the Universe.

Now envision yourself in a tranquil garden setting. Flowers, plants and bushes of every variety create a feast for the eyes and spirit. Colors of every shade and hue, both soft and vibrant, fill you with a sense of peace and joy. Fragrances waft on the gentle breeze, while the sun sparkles through the trees. This is **The Present Moment.** *Allow yourself some precious time to let its beauty permeate all of your senses.*

As beautiful as everything is, though, you're eager to follow the tree-lined path you see at the far side of the garden. It, too, is abundant with natural beauty.

Notice the firm support of the earth under your feet as you're walking.

Feel the gentle breeze as it touches your face and arms.

Observe the vibrant colors of all the bushes and flowers you see along the way. Smell their delightful fragrances. Notice the shapes and sizes of any rocks and stones, and feel the smoothness or roughness of their textures. Hear the clean, clear, fresh water running in a nearby brook or stream.

Feel yourself being the joyful, balanced, well grounded person you truly are at the very center of your being.

Allow yourself to experience your gifts of inner beauty, inner strength, and inner wisdom.

Know that in your spirit you're a beautiful reflection of the One who created you.

As you approach the end of this path, you discover that it's led you right into one of your favorite places where you like to spend time. This may be a place in nature like a park, an out of the way mountain top, a far away island with a majestic waterfall, near a river where you enjoy watching the rapids, at a secluded beach, or any other place of beauty and serenity. It may also be a make-believe place which no one else has ever seen, like a space healing station located somewhere in the universe.

Whatever place you choose, it's always one where you feel very safe and secure, and just being there calms your spirit, or sends it soaring with joy. This is the place we call **The Now.**

Find a comfortable place to sit and allow yourself time to absorb every detail in all of the beauty that surrounds you. Notice the light . . . the colors . . . the fragrances . . . the sounds . . . the sizes . . . the shapes . . . the textures. Look . . . listen . . . touch . . . enjoy. Let yourself become intimately familiar with everything about your special place.

As you bask in this beautiful paradise, remember that this is your safe place. You may come here anytime you need to relax. No one else is allowed here unless you offer a special invitation.

Quietly remain in **The Now** *enjoying the peace and tranquility of this special place for as long as you wish.*

Then notice that, in addition to a bridge on your left, and another bridge on your right, there's also a bridge off in the distance in the center.

Since you want to meet with your pet who's already in Spirit, walk forward toward the center bridge, which is not so very far ahead of you. Pay close attention to everything around you in **The Now** *as you go. Smell the fragrances in the air . . . observe the wide variety of colors . . . reach out and touch anything you wish so that you can feel its texture. Experience everything with all of your senses. Feel the complete sense of serenity and peacefulness.*

As you come closer to the bridge, you realize it glows with light. You're also aware that it curves, so that at first, you can only see half of it. Yet you know intuitively that you'll be able to see the rest of it when you reach the top.

Looking down at where you're walking, the first things you notice are wide bands of brilliant colors. The color of each band changes as you look from left to right—violet, indigo, blue, green, yellow, orange and red.

You understand that you're now on **The Rainbow Bridge***. As you begin to walk across it, you realize how different it feels from an ordinary bridge. It's soft as cotton, yet very sturdy. It almost feels as if it has a vibration of its own, like the hum of a musical instrument being strummed. You feel a wonderful sense of eagerness to cross over it.*

You're peacefully aware that you're the only soul who's on the bridge at the moment and you feel perfectly safe surrounded as you are by the light. You're a welcome visitor, but you also realize that you have only a temporary pass to be here.

As you continue to walk across **The Rainbow Bridge***, you'll see an incredible scene unfold before you, which you might never have expected. On the far side of the bridge, there's a magnificent view of green fields, trees, plants and flowers where all kinds of animals are intermingling together. There are no more hunters or hunted. There are no more foes or enemies. There are only friends.*

Once you've arrived, continue walking and enjoying the peacefulness of all of the animals. Let each one of your senses be fully aware of the magnificent surroundings in which you now find yourself. Let the beauty of it permeate all of your senses.

You may suddenly see one or more of your animal friends coming toward you, greeting you with great anticipation and delight.

Sit anywhere you like, and enjoy saying hello to each and every one of them.

Take this opportunity to ask them all of your questions. You may receive an answer right away, though sometimes you may not. Know that whether you do or don't, it's for the Highest Good of All.

If anything was left unsaid before your pet made his or her transition, this is the time to say it.

If you need forgiveness for something you did, or didn't do, ask for it now.

If you'd like to have another opportunity to make your pet's experience special, ask if he or she would consider reincarnation, now or in the future. If not, don't pressure your pet. Just accept whatever he or she says.

Remain in this peaceful and serene place for as long as you like.

When you feel your questions have all been answered, or that no other information is forthcoming, you can say goodbye for now to all of your friends, with the promise that you will come back at some other time to visit, and with the understanding that you will see each other again once you make your transition into spirit as well.

Thank them for these moments of spiritual closeness and send them on their way.

Know that you will remember everything that happened while you were visiting, and that you're leaving with a new and deeper understanding of your precious animal friends.

Then walk back across the beautiful green field, toward the bridge, enjoying every moment of this incredible peace and beauty. When you arrive at **The Rainbow Bridge**, *walk back across the softness of it into* **The Now**.

Experience once again, with each of your senses, all of the beautiful colors, fragrances and familiar sounds of your special place. Reach out and again feel those objects you originally touched on your way toward the bridge. Be fully aware that you've returned once more to your special place in **the Now**.

Spend a few additional quiet, peaceful moments here by yourself. Know that you can return any time you want, and that the joy and beauty you've experienced will always be here for you.

It's then time to say farewell to your special place of peace and serenity in **The Now** *and prepare to return to* **The**

Present Moment *in the tranquil garden, so begin walking back along the path that originally brought you here.*

Continue to experience all of the vibrant colors, fragrant scents, and beautiful sights. Notice again the textures, shapes and sizes of the rocks and stones you observed when you first walked this path . . . hear the sound of the water in the brook or stream fading more and more softly into the distance.

Follow the path until you arrive back in the peaceful garden where you began this journey. Enjoy the beauty once again, but only for a few moments this time, because you're now ready to return to your normal state of awareness.

Feel yourself in your sitting position once again. Let the roots you put down into Mother Earth recede back into the soles of your feet. Visualize how they're absorbed perfectly back inside of your body as they become smaller and smaller. Wiggle your toes and become even more consciously aware of your body.

Give thanks for the beautiful healing energy that surrounds and permeates every part of your being. Then let it travel upward and exit through the top of your head. See how it blends into the heavens and know that it will always be there for you anytime you need it.

Now become completely aware of your physical body and the present time. Stretch luxuriously, feeling rested and joyful.

Breathe deeply and give thanks.

If necessary, count from one to five, becoming much more alert, aware, and physically active with each successive number . . . and when you're ready, open your eyes.

Chapter 16

In Loving Memory

Chop Chop, one of my beloved Shih-Tzu friends, taught me many important lessons throughout the 14 wonderful years we spent together.

As I was writing this third book, he taught me one final lesson I'd like to share with you—the lesson of letting go.

Even with all of my research and knowledge, and knowing about all of the possibilities for healing which this series of books contains, I wasn't able to offer him even one more day of quality life.

I realized that when the time does come, sometimes it comes so swiftly that we don't have the opportunity to use any healing methods at all. We simply have to accept the fact that the time has come for our pets to leave, and the most loving thing we can do is to let them go.

Chop Chop seemed to be doing fine, or so I thought. Then one day, he was gone. All I could think was: but he was fine yesterday, he was fine last week. What happened?

I was preparing to leave for a book tour in South America and wanted to make sure Chop Chop had enough medicine to last while I was away, so I called my vet and asked for a prescription refill. However, a year had passed since his last blood test, so the vet suggested I bring him in for routine tests just to be sure nothing else needed attention prior to my trip.

On Monday, the urine test came back with satisfactory results, but the blood tests showed fairly high levels of calcium. The vet told me that this could mean any number of things, including kidney trouble or even a tumor. We arranged for an appointment on Tuesday to take some x-rays.

Those pictures revealed that Chop Chop had many stones in both of his kidneys, and about twenty stones clustered in his bladder. Five of them were ready to pass through the urinary tract.

On closer inspection of the x-rays, we could see three stones already embedded in the urethra, but they couldn't be passed on through because of their size. If they weren't removed surgically, he would die within a few days.

After the x-rays were taken, Chop Chop seemed to stop being his brave self any longer. It was almost as if he was saying, "Well, now you know, and I don't have to continue putting up a brave front."

For the remainder of that day, I observed that he wasn't able to rest easily, he had a problem lying down, and he'd frequently move from place to place, obviously trying to find somewhere comfortable to settle down. By Tuesday night he was moaning, and he wasn't able to "find a spot" when we went for our walk.

On Tuesday he also stopped eating, although he'd always been the kind of dog who'd lived for food and treats. He stopped sleeping too, where previously he'd slept 20 hours a day. But Tuesday night, nobody slept, even though his discomfort was somewhat relieved with heavy pain medication.

I wanted a second opinion about his condition, so on Wednesday morning we drove the distance to see my favorite vet and friend, Dr. Sigdestad. Dr. Sig, as I call him, clearly laid out our options.

Chop Chop could undergo surgery on his urethra, an operation that would last about 2 hours. But because he was just one month short of his 14th birthday, and because so many stones would still be in his kidneys and bladder, chances of a satisfactory recovery were very slim. The recuperation time would take about a month, maybe longer, and he would need special care, and a special diet for the rest of his life, which might or might not keep more stones from forming.

I knew immediately that having him undergo surgery of that nature was not the loving thing to do for him. I was going to be leaving for five weeks, and even though he'd still have plenty of loving care and attention at home, I also knew that both the physical and emotional toll he'd have to go through would make it much too difficult for him to endure such an ordeal with any quality of life.

At that moment, it became very clear to me. I finally had to make one of the hardest decisions of my life, but it was a decision

I'd promised him long ago that, if necessary, I'd make for him when the time came.

Yes, it did happen quickly—almost too quickly for me to even fully realize right away that his condition was terminal. And definitely too fast to use any alternative healing therapies in one last effort to save his life.

His departure was swift, but he wanted it that way. I know it was his final gift to me to leave quickly, without lingering, and without giving me false hope. I know the timing was right. And I'm certain that it was what he wanted. I'd told him many times that I wouldn't let him suffer, and he trusted me. He had faith in me, and I couldn't let him down when he was clearly ready to go.

Yes, my heart is grieving for the loss of my precious friend, but I will heal. He taught me that it's important for us to let go when it's time, and he taught me to always find joy in living life fully. I couldn't have asked for a better teacher from whom to learn these two very important lessons.

In loving memory, this book is dedicated to you, my FRIEND and TEACHER!

⌘

CHOP CHOP
3/17/92 – 2/22/06

⌘

Epilogue

The series, *For Pet's Sake, Do Something!*, fulfills my dream of writing three books designed to help you come to the aid of your pets whenever they're faced with various distresses or health challenges.

The first book of this series, *How To Communicate With Your Pets and Help Them Heal*, has introduced you to the importance of intuition and the art of meditation, taught you how to carry on a conversation with your pets by using picture telepathy, and introduced you to a number of spiritual and energetic healing methods, plus guided meditations, which you can use for the benefit of your pets.

The second book, *How To Heal Your Pets Using Nutrition, Herbs and Supplements*, will be published as an e-book in 2007. It will provide you with a wealth of ideas about how to use fresh whole natural foods, vitamins, minerals, herbs, and other nutritional supplements to improve the overall health of your pets, or even help them recover from some serious health challenges. It will also include information about a variety of foods that pets should avoid, as well as recipes for pets with special needs.

The third book of the series, *How To Heal Your Pets Using Alternative Therapies* should also be ready for publication as an e-book later in 2007. It will offer you information about a variety of alternative healing methods including the use of homeopathy, flower essences, incense, essential oils, crystals, color, sound, massage, magnets, hydrotherapy, acupressure, acupuncture and chiropractic.

There are also chapters about pre-testing remedies before you try them; how dogs age; what you need to have in an emergency kit and what you need to know about some emergency first aid procedures; as well as how to provide for your pet's future if something unexpected happens to you.

Ever since my own dog, Chop Chop, clearly told me I needed to *Do Something* when he first lay dying at the age of two, I've wanted to share the many successful methods I've discovered along the way with as many people as possible. Completing these three books is a special part of my Life Assignment, and it gives me great joy to know that you, too, are now empowered to *Do Something* for your own beloved pets!

Dr. Monica Diedrich
Anaheim, California, USA
www.petcommunicator.com

About the Author

Monica Diedrich knew that she could hear animals speak ever since she was eight years old. By the time she was 18, she had also begun to share the gift of her insight and guidance with humans, helping them with their life challenges, as well. Since 1990, however, her work has been devoted *exclusively* to the well-being of animals.

She holds the degree of Doctor of Metaphysics and is an ordained minister. Studying Eastern traditions developed her understanding of the natural interconnection between humans and animals, as well as demonstrating the importance of attaining healing at all three levels—physically, emotionally and spiritually.

In addition to providing both introductory and private consultations, Dr. Monica presents seminars, teaches classes, and writes books about the art of animal communication. She is also a regular contributor to several TV shows, including one aired in South Korea.

Her first book, *What Your Animals Tell Me*, has won two awards: the 2001 National Self-Published Book Awards from *Writer's Digest*; and the 2003 Nonfiction Award, Farmer's Market Online, "Direct from the Author Book Award," first place. It has also been translated and released in several other languages, among them, Spanish, Japanese and Croatian. Her second book, *Pets Have Feelings Too!* was an award winning finalist in the Animals/Pets:General category of the USA BookNews Best Books 2006 National Awards and was listed on USABookNews.com for five months.

A native of Argentina, Monica has lived in Southern California for over 35 years with her husband and children, both human and pet. She can be reached directly through her informational website at http://www.petcommunicator.com.

Breinigsville, PA USA
08 October 2009
225482BV00002B/2/A